Christian Grün

Storing and Querying Large XML Instances

Christian Grün

Storing and Querying Large XML Instances

Design of a full-fledged XML storage and query architecture

Südwestdeutscher Verlag für Hochschulschriften

Imprint
Any brand names and product names mentioned in this book are subject to trademark, brand or patent protection and are trademarks or registered trademarks of their respective holders. The use of brand names, product names, common names, trade names, product descriptions etc. even without a particular marking in this work is in no way to be construed to mean that such names may be regarded as unrestricted in respect of trademark and brand protection legislation and could thus be used by anyone.

Publisher:
Südwestdeutscher Verlag für Hochschulschriften
is a trademark of
Dodo Books Indian Ocean Ltd., member of the OmniScriptum S.R.L Publishing group
str. A.Russo 15, of. 61, Chisinau-2068, Republic of Moldova Europe
Printed at: see last page
ISBN: 978-3-8381-2459-9

Zugl. / Approved by: Konstanz, Universität, Diss., 2010

Copyright © Christian Grün
Copyright © 2011 Dodo Books Indian Ocean Ltd., member of the OmniScriptum S.R.L Publishing group

Abstract

After its introduction in 1998, XML has quickly emerged as the *de facto* exchange format for textual data. Only ten years later, the amount of information that is being processed day by day, locally and globally, has virtually exploded, and no end is in sight. Correspondingly, many XML documents and collections have become much too large for being retrieved in their raw form – and this is where database technology gets into the game.

This thesis describes the design of a full-fledged XML storage and query architecture, which represents the core of the Open Source database system BASEX. In contrast to numerous other works on XML processing, which either focus on theoretical aspects or practical implementation details, we have tried to bring the two worlds together: well-established and novel concepts from *database technology* and *compiler construction* are consolidated to a powerful and extensible software architecture that is supposed to both withstand the demands of complex *real-life applications* and comply with all the intricacies of the *W3C Recommendations*.

In the *Storage* chapter, existing tree encodings are explored, which allow XML documents to be mapped to a database. The *Pre/Dist/Size* triple is chosen as the most suitable encoding and further optimized by *merging* all XML node properties into a single tuple, *compactifying* redundant information, and *inlining* attributes and numeric values. The address ranges of numerous large-scale and real-life XML instances are analyzed to find an optimal tradeoff between maximum document and minimum database size. The process of building a database is described in detail, including the import of tree data other than XML and the creation of main memory database instances. As one of the distinguishing features, the resulting storage is enriched by light-weight structural, value and full-text indexes, which speed up query processing by orders of magnitudes.

The *Querying* chapter is introduced with a survey on state of the art XML query languages. We give some insight into the design of an *XQuery processor* and then focus on the *optimization* of queries. Beside classical concepts, such as *constant folding* or *static typing*, many optimizations are specific to XML: location paths are rewritten to access less XML nodes, and FLWOR expressions are reorganized to reduce the algorithmic complexity. A unique feature of our query processor represents the dynamic rewriting of location paths to take advantage of available *index structures*. Next, we examine the evaluation of queries and propose an *adaptive* approach to benefit from both the *iterative* and *atomic* processing paradigm. Based on the evaluation of location paths, it is illustrated how databases are accessed by the query processor. The concluding summary gives an overview on the optimizations that have been applied to the most important XQuery expressions.

In the *Performance* chapter, we demonstrate the efficiency and scalability of the resulting database system BASEX. The storage and query capabilities are tested and compared with other database systems and query processors. The benchmark results show that the proposed architecture and its interplay between the storage and query components embraces some qualities that are, to the best of our knowledge, unique and unprecedented among comparable products.

Zusammenfassung (German Abstract)

Nachdem XML 1998 das Licht der Welt erblickt hat, hat es sich sehr schnell zum *Quasi-Standard* für den Austausch textueller Daten entwickelt. Nur zehn Jahre später sind die Informationsmengen, die tagtäglich lokal und global verarbeitet werden, explodiert, und ein Ende der Entwicklung ist noch nicht abzusehen. Demzufolge sind auch viele XML-Dokumente und -Kollektionen längst zu groß geworden, um Sie in ihrer Rohform abzufragen – und hier kommt Datenbanktechnologie zum Einsatz.

Diese Dissertation beschreibt das Design einer ausgereiften XML-Speicher- und Query-Architektur, die zugleich den Kern des Open-Source Datenbanksystems BaseX darstellt. Im Gegensatz zu zahlreichen anderen Publikationen über XML, die sich entweder theoretischen Teilaspekten oder praktischen Implementierungsdetails verschreiben, wurde in dieser Arbeit versucht, beide Welten zusammenzuführen: wohlbekannte und neuartige Konzepte der *Datenbanktechnologie* und des *Compiler-Baus* bilden die Basis für eine mächtige und offene Software-Architektur, die sowohl den Anforderungen komplexer, *realer Anwendungen* standhalten als auch die Feinheiten der *W3C-Empfehlungen* berücksichtigen und einhalten soll.

Im *Storage*-Kapitel werden existierende Baum-Kodierungen untersucht, die die Speicherung von XML-Dokumenten in Datenbanken ermöglichen. Das *Pre/Dist/Size*-Tripel wird als die geeignetste Kodierung ausgewählt und weiter optimiert: alle Eigenschaften eines XML-Knotens werden in *einem Tupel* abgebildet, redundante Information werden *kompaktifiziert* und Attribute und numerische Werte werden *gelinzt*, d.h. direkt innerhalb der Tupel abgespeichert. Die Adressbereiche zahlreicher großer, realer XML-Instanzen werden analysiert, um einen optimalen Kompromiss zwischen maximaler Dokument- und minimaler Datenbankgröße zu finden. Die Erzeugung neuer Datenbankinstanzen wird im Detail vorgestellt; dabei werden auch hauptspeicherorientierte Datenbanken und andere hierarchische Datentypen neben XML betrachtet. Eine Besonderheit der diskutierten Speicherarchitektur stellt die Erweiterung durch schlanke struktur-, inhalts- und volltextbasierte Indexstrukturen dar, die die Anfragegeschwindigkeit um mehrere Größenordnungen beschleunigen können.

Das *Querying*-Kapitel beginnt mit einem Überblick über die relevanten XML-Anfragesprachen und beschreibt den Aufbau eines *XQuery-Prozessors*. Die *Optimierung* von Anfragen steht anschließend im Mittelpunkt. Klassische Techniken wie *Constant Folding* oder *Statische Typisierung* werden durch XML-spezifische Optimierungen ergänzt: Dokumentpfade werden umgeschrieben, um die Zahl der adressierten XML-Knoten zu reduzieren, und FLWOR-Ausdrücke werden reorganisiert, um die algorithmischen Kosten zu senken. Ein einzigartiges Feature des vorgestellten Query-Prozessors stellt die flexible Umschreibung von Dokumentpfaden für indexbasierte Anfragen dar. Als nächstes wird die Evaluierung von Anfragen untersucht und ein adaptiver Ansatz vorgestellt, der die Vorteile der *iterativen* und *atomaren* Anfrageverarbeitung vereinigt. Anhand der Evaluierung von Dokumentpfaden wird der Zugriff auf die Datenbank veranschaulicht. Der abschließende Überblick fasst die Optimierungsschritte zusammen, die auf die wichtigsten XQuery-Ausdrücke angewandt wurden.

Die Effizienz und Skalierbarkeit des Datenbanksystems BASEX ist Schwerpunkt des *Performance*-Kapitels. Die Speicher- und Anfrage-Architektur wird getrennt voneinander analysiert und mit anderen Datenbank-Systemen und Query-Prozessoren verglichen. Die Ergebnisse sollen demonstrieren, dass die vorgestellte Architektur und das Zusammenspiel zwischen den Speicher- und Query-Komponenten über bestimmte Qualitäten verfügt, die unserem Kenntnisstand nach einzigartig unter vergleichbaren Produkten sind.

Acknowledgments

Most certainly, this thesis would not have been completed without the continuous help, support and inspirations of some persons, which I am pleased to mention in the following:

First of all, I owe my deepest gratitude to my supervisor Marc H. Scholl, who has given me all the time and freedom I could have possibly asked for to develop and pursue my own ideas – a privilege that I know many postgraduates can only dream of. At the same time, Marc has always had time for discussions, and I learned a lot from both his guidance and vast expertise. Whenever I had doubts whether I was on the right path – or any path at all – it was Marc who backed me, and confirmed me to go on.

Next, I would like to thank Marcel Waldvogel and his `disy` Group. The exchange between his and our group consisted in numerous fruitful debates, joint publications and, as I believe, brought the work of all of us forward more quickly. Another thank you is directed to Harald Reiterer, who was the first in Konstanz to get me enthusiastic about scientific work. The cooperation between his HCI Group and ours lasts till the present day.

It was my colleague Alexander Holupirek who I shared most prolific ideas with during the last years, and some more drinks in the evenings. He gave me regular feedback on my flights of fancy (or figments), and many of the contributions presented in this work are due to his invaluable inspirations. I am also indebted to Marc Kramis, whose visionary approach has advised me to remain open for new ideas, and Sebastian Graf, who has triggered our most recent cooperation with the `disy` Group.

The collaboration with all the students working in my project was one of the most fulfilling experiences, and I learnt a lot about what it means to lead a project, and how productive *real* team work can be. In particular, I'd like to say thank you to Volker Wildi, Tim Petrowski, Sebastian Gath, Bastian Lemke, Lukas Kircher, Andreas Weiler, Jörg Hauser, Michael Seiferle, Sebastian Faller, Wolfgang Miller, Elmedin Dedović, Lukas Lewandowski, Oliver Egli, Leonard Wörteler, Rositsa Shadura, Dimitar Popov, Jens Erat, and Patrick Lang. I have chosen a somewhat chronological order, assuming that all of you know how much I value your individual contributions. Another big thank you goes to Barbara Lüthke, our secretary with excellent language skills who deliberately spent countless hours proof-reading the entire thesis.

Last but not least, words cannot express my appreciation to my parents, my brother Achim, and Milda. Your endless emotional support was the real driving force behind this work. To give it at least another try: *Danke* and *Ačiū*!

Contents

1	**Introduction**	**1**
	1.1 Motivation	1
	1.2 Contribution	2
	1.3 Outline	3
	1.4 Publications	4
2	**Storage**	**5**
	2.1 Introduction	5
	2.2 History	5
	2.3 XML Encodings	7
	2.3.1 Document Object Model	7
	2.3.2 Pre- and Postorder	8
	2.3.3 Level Depth	10
	2.3.4 Number of Descendants	10
	2.3.5 Parent Reference	11
	2.3.6 Node Properties	12
	2.3.7 Namespaces	13
	2.4 Pre/Dist/Size Mapping	14
	2.4.1 Address Ranges	15
	2.4.1.1 Analysis	15
	2.4.1.2 XML Instances	17
	2.4.2 Table Mapping	19
	2.4.2.1 Attribute Inlining	19
	2.4.2.2 Bit Ranges	20
	2.4.2.3 Compactification	21
	2.4.2.4 Integer Inlining	21
	2.4.2.5 Updates	23
	2.5 Database Architecture	25
	2.5.1 Database Construction	25

Contents

  2.5.2 Generic Parsing 28
  2.5.3 Main Memory vs Persistent Storage 29
 2.6 Index Structures 31
  2.6.1 Names 31
  2.6.2 Path Summary 33
  2.6.3 Values 35
    2.6.3.1 Compression 36
    2.6.3.2 Construction 36
    2.6.3.3 Main Memory Awareness 37
  2.6.4 Full-Texts 37
    2.6.4.1 Fuzzy Index 39
    2.6.4.2 Trie Index 40

3 Querying   **43**
 3.1 XML Languages 43
  3.1.1 XPath 44
  3.1.2 XQuery 46
  3.1.3 XQuery Full Text 47
  3.1.4 XQuery Update 49
 3.2 Query Processing 50
  3.2.1 Analysis 50
  3.2.2 Compilation 52
  3.2.3 Evaluation 52
  3.2.4 Serialization 53
 3.3 Optimizations 53
  3.3.1 Static Optimizations 54
    3.3.1.1 Constant Folding/Propagation 54
    3.3.1.2 Variable/Function Inlining 56
    3.3.1.3 Dead Code Elimination 57
    3.3.1.4 Static Typing 58
    3.3.1.5 Location Path Rewritings 59
    3.3.1.6 FLWOR expressions 61
  3.3.2 Index Optimizations 64
    3.3.2.1 Database Context 65
    3.3.2.2 Predicate Analysis 66
    3.3.2.3 Path Inversion 68

		3.3.3	Runtime Optimizations	70

- 3.3.3 Runtime Optimizations 70
    - 3.3.3.1 Direct Sequence Access 71
    - 3.3.3.2 General Comparisons 72
- 3.4 Evaluation 73
    - 3.4.1 Iterative Processing 74
        - 3.4.1.1 Caching 76
        - 3.4.1.2 Adaptive Approach 78
        - 3.4.1.3 Expressions 81
    - 3.4.2 Location Paths 83
        - 3.4.2.1 Staircase Join 84
        - 3.4.2.2 Path Traversal 86
        - 3.4.2.3 Optimizations 90
- 3.5 Summary 92
- 3.6 Examples 100
    - 3.6.1 Index Access 100
    - 3.6.2 XMark 101

4 Performance 107
- 4.1 Storage 108
- 4.2 Querying 111
    - 4.2.1 XQuery 113
    - 4.2.2 XMark 116
        - 4.2.2.1 Main Memory Processing 116
        - 4.2.2.2 Database Processing 118
        - 4.2.2.3 XMark Queries 122
    - 4.2.3 XQuery Full Text 126
- 4.3 Statistics 130

5 Conclusion 133

Appendix 135
- Bibliography 135
- List of Figures 146
- List of Tables 148

1 Introduction

1.1 Motivation

"XML is bulky", "XML processing is slow", "XML documents are small": my first encounters with XML would never have pointed into the direction which I have pursued for the past years. XML, the Extensible Markup Language introduced by the W3 Consortium in 1998 [BPSM+08], evolved from the SGML ISO standard. The initial notion was to offer a generic meta markup language for documents. Since then, XML has become a de facto standard for the industrial and scientific exchange of *textual* information.

XML allows for a hierarchic mapping of contents by representing all data in a tree structure. This flexibility led to challenges – and preconceptions – that were unfamiliar to the world of relational databases:

- **XML is bulky?** Indeed: meta data in XML documents, which are encoded as element names, attributes, comments or processing instructions, can result in a verbose representation.

- **XML processing is slow?** Compared to tabular data, the processing of hierarchic structures is not straight-forward and demands more sophisticated query algorithms.

As a first consequence, XML documents were considered to be a suitable format for handling small amounts of data, but dismissed for database storage. If we regard the situation in 2010 – twelve years after the publication of the first edition of the XML Recommendation – this has drastically changed: The strict limitations of two-dimensional tabular data have been more and more abandoned to give way to the paradigm of *semistructured data* [Abi97, Bun97]. Numerous DBMS are now available that support, or are specialized in, the storage of large XML instances. Big players like DB2 and Oracle offer native storage of XML documents, and many free and commercial text corpora – such as Wikipedia, SwissProt or MedLine, all occupying several gigabytes of raw data – are distributed via XML.

1.2. Contribution

A language for searching such large amounts of data was the next task. Many efforts have been made to query XML documents [AQM+97, DFF+99, CRF00], and XPath [CD99] and XQuery [BCF+07] have become the official W3C Recommendations. While most of these approaches focus on the structure, it has been observed that many instances are rather *document-centric*, containing mixed content and full-texts [BBB00]. As a result, language extensions have been proposed to bring the database and information retrieval world closer together [TW02, GSBS03, TS04, BSAY04], a development which eventually led to the definition of the W3C XQuery and XPath Full Text Candidate Recommendation [AYBB+09]. Similar to SQL, update statements are essential in database languages. First attempts described in [LM03], [TIHW01] and [SHS04] eventually ended up in the XQuery Update Candidate Recommendation [CDF+09]. The success of XML has led to quite a number of other specifications, ranging from the early XSL Transformation language [Cla99] to the upcoming Scripting Extension [CEF+08].

1.2 Contribution

In a nutshell, this thesis is about the storage and query architecture of a full-fledged native XML database. While this might not be the first attempt, we believe that a major contribution of this work is the thorough consideration and consequent consolidation of both theoretical and practical aspects. Over the past years, we have observed that numerous theoretical approaches have failed to reach a mature level, as the proposed ideas could not cope with the complexity of real-life demands. As an example, optimizations for basic features of XPath and XQuery could not be scaled and adopted to complex query expressions. At the same time, many existing implementations would clearly yield much better performance and scalability if they were based on a solid theoretical foundation (to quote Kurt Lewin: "There is nothing more practical than a good theory." [Lew51]). In this work, we have tried to bring the two worlds closer together. All concepts were scrutinized not only for their efficiency and scalability, but also for their universality. Accordingly, the resulting database architecture was supposed to:

- withstand the demands of real workloads and complex applications,
- comply with all the subtleties and intricacies of the W3C Recommendations, and
- show unique performance and scalability.

Single contributions have been summarized in the Conclusion (Chapter 5).

1.3 Outline

The work is structured as follows:

- **Chapter 2** starts off with a short *historical overview* of XML storage techniques. Various tree encodings are analyzed, and the *Pre/Dist/Size* encoding, which is chosen as favorite, is presented in more detail. Real-life, large-scale XML documents and collections are examined to get a feeling for the optimal tradeoff between maximum document and minimum database size. Various optimizations are then performed on the encoding, including the *merge* of all XML node properties into a single tuple, the *compactification* of redundant information, and the *inlining* of attributes and numerical values in the tuple. Next, the process of *constructing* a database is illustrated step by step. Additional *indexes* are proposed as a complement to the main database structures to speedup both structural and content-based queries.

- **Chapter 3** is introduced with a survey on the most relevant XML query languages. Some insight into the design of an *XQuery processor* is given, followed by a section on static and dynamic query optimizations. Beside classical compiler concepts, such as *Constant Folding*, *Dead Code Elimination* or *Static Typing*, XML specific optimizations are described, including the rewriting of *FLWOR expressions* and *location paths*. Special attention is directed to expressions that can be rewritten for *index access*. Next, an *adaptive* approach is proposed for query evaluation, which combines the advantages of the *iterative* and *atomic* processing paradigm. An extra section is devoted to the database-supported traversal of location paths. The chapter is concluded with a summary, highlighting the optimizations of the most important XQuery expressions, and the presentation of some original and optimized query plans.

- **Chapter 4** demonstrates that the proposed architecture yields excellent performance and scalability: both the storage and query capabilities are tested and compared with competing systems.

BASEX, an Open Source XML database system, is the practical offspring of this thesis [GHK+06, GGHS09b, Grü10]. The deliberate focus on a real-life system with a steadily growing user community allowed us to benefit from a wide range of real-life scenarios, and to continuously review and ponder the usefulness of new software features. In retrospect, feedback from the Open Source community was a decisive factor in the development of BASEX.

1.4 Publications

The following texts were published as a result of this research project:

1. Sebastian Graf, Lukas Lewandowski, and Christian Grün. JAX-RX – Unified REST Access to XML Resources. Technical Report, KN-2010-DiSy-01, University of Konstanz, Germany, June 2010
2. Christian Grün, Sebastian Gath, Alexander Holupirek, and Marc H. Scholl. INEX Efficiency Track meets XQuery Full Text in BaseX. In *Pre-Proceedings of the 8th INEX Workshop*, pages 192–197, 2009
3. Christian Grün, Sebastian Gath, Alexander Holupirek, and Marc H. Scholl. XQuery Full Text Implementation in BaseX. In *XSym*, volume 5679 of *Lecture Notes in Computer Science*, pages 114–128. Springer, 2009
4. Alexander Holupirek, Christian Grün, and Marc H. Scholl. BaseX & DeepFS – Joint Storage for Filesystem and Database. In *EDBT*, volume 360 of *ACM International Conference Proceedings Series*, pages 1108–1111. ACM, 2009
5. Christian Grün, Alexander Holupirek, and Marc H. Scholl. Visually Exploring and Querying XML with BaseX. In *BTW*, volume 103 of *LNI*, pages 629–632. GI, 2007
6. Christian Grün, Alexander Holupirek, and Marc H. Scholl. Melting Pot XML – Bringing File Systems and Databases One Step Closer. In *BTW*, volume 103 of *LNI*, pages 309–323. GI, 2007
7. Christian Grün, Alexander Holupirek, Marc Kramis, Marc H. Scholl, and Marcel Waldvogel. Pushing XPath Accelerator to its Limits. In *ExpDB*. ACM 2006
8. Christian Grün. Pushing XML Main Memory Databases to their Limits. In *Grundlagen von Datenbanken*. Institute of Computer Science, Martin-Luther-University, 2006

BASEX contains numerous other features that are only partially reflected in this thesis, or not at all. The client-/server architecture is presented in Weiler's master thesis [Wei10]; details on the XQuery Full Text implementation are covered in Gath's master thesis [Gat09], and Kircher's bachelor thesis gives some insight into the implementation of XQuery Update [Kir10]. As an addition, a user-friendly GUI interface contains several query facilities and visualizations and offers a tight coupling between the visual frontend and the database backend (see [GHS07], or Hauser's bachelor thesis for details on the TreeMap visualization [Hau09]).

2 Storage

2.1 Introduction

XML documents are based on tree structures. Trees are connected acyclic graphs; as such, they need specialized storage structures, which will be discussed in this chapter. Section 2.2 gives a short introduction to the historical development of XML storage techniques, Section 2.3 will analyze various XML encodings, and Section 2.4 will present the Pre/Dist/Size encoding and its optimizations in depth. An overview on the proposed database architecture is given in Section 2.5, and Section 2.6 will conclude the chapter with the description of additional light-weight index structures, which will speed up many queries by orders of magnitudes.

2.2 History

Semi-structured data, as defined by [Abi97] and [Bun97], came into play when relational database systems were the standard storage technology, and object-oriented databases were in the limelight. STORED (Semistructured TO RElational Data) was one of the first systems that focused on the storage of semi-structured documents [DFS99]. The proposed algorithm to analyze the input data was inspired by data mining techniques. Regularities in the data were utilized to define a relational schema. The database structure resulted in a *mixed schema*, containing relational tables for regular data and graphs to store remaining, irregular structures. This approach worked out particularly well for regular data instances, but reached its limits if the input was primarily irregular.

Even before, another system to enter the stage was LORE [MAG$^+$97]. The "Lightweight Object Repository" was based on the Object Exchange Model (OEM). OEM was introduced by TSIMMIS [PGMW95], another system developed in Stanford; it served as a unified data model for representing and exchanging semi-structured data between different systems. The textual OEM interchange format, as defined in [GCCM98], offered a simple way to manually edit and modify existing data structures.

2.2. History

While many features were rather classical, the great benefit of LORE was that it did not enforce a pre-defined schema on the input data. The underlying storage allowed all incoming data instances to have different structures. The idea to operate without schema on the data (i.e., *schema-oblivious*, [KKN03]) differed fundamentally from traditional, relational database systems, which postulated a "schema first" approach. Another interesting and still up-to-date feature of the LORE architecture, such as DataGuides [GW97], will be discussed in more detail in 2.6.2.

NATIX [KM00] was one of the first engines to incorporate the tree structure of semi-structured data in its underlying physical storage. A tree storage manager was applied to map complete and partial documents (subtrees) into low-level record units. Three types of records were defined: *aggregate* nodes represented inner nodes of a tree, *literal* nodes contained raw document contents, and *proxy* nodes were used to reference different records for larger documents. In contrast to other approaches, database updates were already taken into consideration; depending on the number of expected occupancy of records, the maintenance policy could be fine-tuned.

In [FK99], Florescu and Kossmann analyzed various approaches for mapping XML data to tables in relational database management systems (RDBMS), all schema-oblivious. All element nodes were labeled with a unique *oid*. The *Edge* table referenced all edges of a document by storing the source oid, a target reference, the edge label and an ordinal number, which denoted the original order of the target nodes. A second, *Binary* mapping scheme, inspired by [vZAW99], grouped all nodes with the same label into one table, and the third *Universal* scheme, which corresponds to a full outer join of Binary tables, stored all edges and contents in a single table. Two alternative ways were proposed to store attribute values and text nodes: depending on the data type, separate value tables were created and linked with the main tables. Alternatively, values were "inlined", i.e., directly stored in the structure tables. A benchmark was performed, using a commercial RBDMS, in which the binary approach with inlined values yielded the best results. Further research has revealed that other storage patterns are often superior to the binary mapping (see e.g. [GC07]). It can be assessed, however, that the general idea to map XML documents to tabular relational table structures has found many supporters, as will be shown in the following.

2.3 XML Encodings

As outlined in the introduction, trees are the underlying structure of XML documents. Tree encodings have a long history in computer science. To map XML trees to another representation, we need to find an encoding $\mathcal{E}$ that matches the following demands:

1. The encoding must be capable of mapping a document to a database and exactly reconstructing the original document ($\mathcal{E}^{-1}$).
2. As node order is essential in semi-structured data, such as full-texts, the encoding must reflect the original node order.
3. Tree traversal is important in XML processing and querying, and must be efficiently supported.

The properties, which will be analyzed in the following, represent single properties of tree nodes. The combination of the properties results in different encodings $\mathcal{E}$, the values of which form tuples. While the tuples can be stored in different ways, we will focus on the two following variants:

1. *set-based*: as a *relation*, i.e., a *set* of tuples, in a database. Here, sets are unordered collections of distinct tuples.
2. *sequential*: as a *sequence* of tuples. In our context, sequences are ordered lists of distinct tuples.

The *set-based* variant will also be called *relational*, as a traditional relational database (RDBMS) with SQL as query language is assumed to exist as backend (see e.g. [STZ+99] or [Gru02]). In contrast, the *sequential* variant will sometimes be referred to as the *native* approach, as it will be based on specially tailored storage structures to support inherent XML characteristics. While the distinction may seem clear at first glance, different approaches exist in practice that cannot be uniquely assigned to either approach: a relational database can be tuned to sequentially process nodes (as pursued by the *Staircase Join* algorithms [GvKT03]), and native database backends can be extended by relational paradigms (as done in the MONETDB database), and so on.

2.3.1 Document Object Model

The DOM, short for *Document Object Model*, is the most popular representation for XML documents. It is used to map XML instances to a main memory tree structure [ABC+99].

2.3. XML Encodings

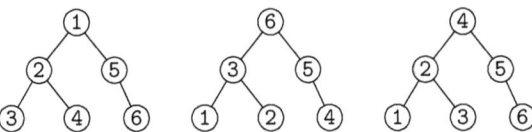

Figure 2.1: Preorder, postorder, and inorder traversal

With its help, the structure and contents of a document can be accessed directly and updated dynamically. All XML nodes are represented as transient objects, which contain direct references to parent and child nodes and have additional properties, dependent on their node kind. While the flexible DOM structure serves well to process smaller documents, many issues arise when data has to be permanently stored. Some early, discontinued approaches for persistently storing DOM can be found in [HM99, EH00].

2.3.2 Pre- and Postorder

It was Knuth in his well-known monograph [Knu68] who coined the terms *preorder*, *postorder* and *inorder* to describe different traversals of binary trees (see Figure 2.1). By nature, tree traversals are defined in a recursive manner. In preorder, the root node is visited first. Next, a preorder traversal is performed on all child nodes from left to right. In postorder, the root is visited after traversing all children, and in inorder, the root is touched after the left and before the right child is traversed. From these traversals, pre- and postorder are relevant in the context of XML, as they are also applicable to trees with more than two children.

Preorder corresponds to the natural *document order*, i.e., the order in which XML nodes are sequentially parsed and new nodes are encountered. Postorder can be sequentially constructed as well if the post value is assigned and incremented every time a node is closed. Hence, both encodings can be assigned in a single run and in linear time. A SAX parser [MB04] can be used to parse XML documents; details are found in 2.5.1.

As depicted in Figure 2.2, *pre* and *post* values of an XML document can be visualized in a two-dimensional coordinate system, the so-called *pre/post plane* [Gru02]. This plane visualizes interesting hierarchical relationships between XML nodes.

Dietz was the first to discover that preorder and postorder can be utilized to determine ancestor and descendant relationships in trees [Die82]: "A vertex x is an ancestor of y iff x occurs before y in the preorder traversal of T and after y in the postorder traversal". This observation was applied to XML and formalized for all XPath axes in Grust's

2.3. XML Encodings

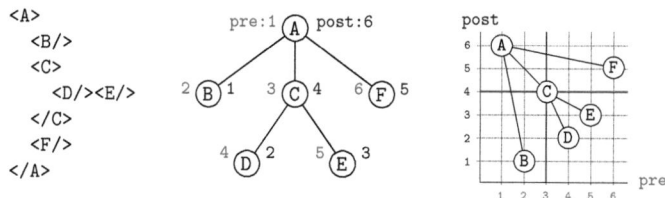

Figure 2.2: XML document, tree with *pre/post* values, *pre/post* plane

XPath Accelerator [Gru02]. Each XML node partitions the plane into four regions, which correspond to four of the XPath axes (see 3.1.1) and have the following properties:

- the *ancestors* n' of a node n are found in the upper, left region:
  $pre(n') < pre(n) \land post(n') > post(n)$
- the *descendants* n' of a node n are in the lower, right region:
  $pre(n') > pre(n) \land post(n') < post(n)$
- *following* nodes (excluding descendants) are in the upper, right region:
  $pre(n') > pre(n) \land post(n') > post(n)$
- *preceding* nodes (excluding ancestors) are in the lower, left region:
  $pre(n') < pre(n) \land post(n') < post(n)$

In Figure 2.2, node C was chosen as n. It has node A as ancestor, D and E as descendants, B as preceding, and F as following node.

Both in set-based and in sequential processing, all operations need constant time if single source nodes n and single target nodes n' are considered. If we want to find all target nodes for a single source node, we need to check the *pre* and *post* values of all nodes of a tree, an operation which results in linear costs. B-Trees and R-Trees can be applied to get better performance [Gru02].

In sequential processing, all nodes can be sorted by their *pre* values. As *pre* values are unique, they can be used as node identifiers (*id* property). Care has to be taken if databases are updated, as *pre* values may change with node deletions or insertions. In the worst case, the whole document will be renumbered. If unique identifiers are needed in a database scenario (e.g., if the same nodes need to be addressed before and after updates), additional, persistent *ids* can be assigned, which will not be affected by database modifications. – The *Staircase Join* algorithms offer an elegant and efficient

2.3. XML Encodings

approach to speed up axis evaluation [GvKT03]. It will be described in more detail in Section 3.4.2.

2.3.3 Level Depth

Not all relationships between XML nodes can be determined exclusively with pre and $post$. The $level$ is another property that represents the depth of a node within a tree, i.e., the length of the path from the root to the given node. It can be used to evaluate four other XPath axes:

- the *parent* n' of a node n is an ancestor, the level of which is smaller by one:
  $pre(n') < pre(n) \land post(n') > post(n) \land level(n') = level(n) - 1$
- the *children* n' of a node n are descendants with a level bigger by one:
  $pre(n') > pre(n) \land post(n') < post(n) \land level(n') = level(n) + 1$
- the *following siblings* n' of a node n are following nodes that have the same parent node p and, hence, are on the same level:
  $pre(n') > pre(n) \land post(n') > post(n) \land post(n') < post(p) \land level(n') = level(n)$
- correspondingly, all preceding nodes with the same parent are the *preceding siblings* n' of a node n:
  $pre(n') < pre(n) \land post(n') < post(n) \land pre(n') > pre(p) \land level(n') = level(n)$

Similar to pre and $post$, the operations can be performed in constant time for single source and target nodes, and linear time is needed for a set-based evaluation of several target nodes.

While the *self* axis in XPath is trivial, the two axes *descendant-or-self* and *ancestor-or-self* are combinations of the existing axes. The evaluation of the remaining *attribute* and *namespace* axes are not considered in this context, as it depends on the specific design of an implementation and does not pose any particular challenges that differ from the existing ones[1].

2.3.4 Number of Descendants

Li and Moon noticed early that the preorder and postorder encoding is expensive when trees are to be updated [LM01]. They proposed an alternative encoding, namely the

---

[1] note that the *namespace* axis has been marked deprecated with XPath 2.0 [CD07]

combination of an *extended preorder* and the *range of descendants*. In the extended preorder, gaps are left for new nodes, and the $size$ property encapsulates the number of descendant nodes. While the proposed encoding leads to new updating issues, which arise as soon as all gaps are filled (costs on updates will be further detailed in Section 2.4.2.5), the $size$ property brings in helpful properties, which are only partially covered in the publication itself:

- n' is a *descendant* of n if
  $pre(n) < pre(n') \leq pre(n) + size(n)$
- n' is the *following sibling* of n if
  $pre(n') = pre(n) + size(n) + 1 \wedge level(n') = level(n)$
- correspondingly, n' is the *preceding sibling* of n if
  $pre(n') = pre(n) - size(n') - 1 \wedge level(n') = level(n)$

A direct relationship exists towards pre, $post$ and $level$. The $size$ property can be calculated as follows [GT04]:

$$size(n) = post(n) - pre(n) + level(n)$$

The $size$ property is particularly beneficial if tuples are sequentially stored and evaluated. As an example, all children of a node can be traversed by a simple loop:

Algorithm 1 ProcessChildren(*node*: Node)
---
1   **for** $c := pre(node) + 1$ **to** $pre(node) + size(node)$ **step** $size(c)$ **do**
2   process child with $c \equiv pre(child)$
3   **end for**

2.3.5 Parent Reference

The parent of a node can be retrieved via pre, $post$ and $level$. This operation is expensive, however, as it results in linear costs, particularly if nodes are stored in a set-based manner and if no additional index structures are created. Obviously, costs for the reverse *parent* and *ancestor* axes can be reduced to constant time if the parent reference is directly stored.

As proposed in [GHK+06, Grü06], the pre value of the parent node can be used as *parent* reference. Four of the XPath axes can now be evaluated as follows:

- n' is a *child* of n if $parent(n') = pre(n)$

2.3. XML Encodings

- n' is a *parent* of n if $pre(n') = parent(n)$
- n' is a *following-sibling* of n if $pre(n') > pre(n) \land parent(n') = parent(n)$
- n' is a *preceding-sibling* of n if $pre(n') < pre(n) \land parent(n') = parent(n)$

In set-based processing, *post* or *size* values are needed to evaluate the *descendant, ancestor, following,* and *preceding* axes. In sequential processing, however, the combination of *pre* and *parent* constitutes a minimal encoding to traverse all existing XPath axes and reconstruct the original document. Next, the *Staircase Join* algorithms can be rewritten to utilize the *parent* property, as will be shown in 3.4.2.

As a slight, yet powerful variation, the absolute parent reference can be replaced with the relative distance to the parent node. In [GGHS09b], it has been shown that this $dist$ property is update-invariant: subtrees preserve their original distance values if they are moved to or inserted in new documents. In contrast, absolute parent references to pre values need to be completely renumbered.

2.3.6 Node Properties

Some other properties are necessary to map XML documents to a database and restore the original representation. Location steps consist of XPath axes, which are further refined by a *kind* test. The *kind* property represents the type of an XML node and can be *document-node, element, attribute, text, comment,* or *processing-instruction*. Each node kind has specific properties that have to be additionally referenced or stored in a database [FMM+07]:

- Each XML document has a non-visible **document node** on top. A document has a unique *document uri* property, which serves as a reference to the original document location. Next, document nodes may have an arbitrary number of *children* (elements, processing instructions, and comments), but only one root element.

- **Elements** contain all contents between an element's start and end tag. Tags are represented by angle brackets (e.g. <name>...</name>). An element has a *name*, a unique *parent*, and an arbitrary number of *children* (elements, processing instructions, comments, and texts) and *attributes*. While children have a fixed order and may contain duplicates, attributes may be serialized in a different order, but their names need to be unique. Next, *namespaces* may be defined for an element node and its descendants.

2.3. XML Encodings

- An **attribute** is *owned* by an element, i.e., its *parent* is always an element. Attributes have a *name* and a *value* and no children. They are serialized within element start tags: `<node name="value"/>`
- **Texts** are usually enclosed by start and end tags. They have a *content* property, which contains the actual textual data: `<...>content</...>`.
- **Processing instructions** can occur all around a document. They are used to keep information for other processors and languages unchanged in an XML document, and they have a *parent*, *target*, and *content* property: `<?target text?>`
- Similar to processing instructions, **comments** may be placed anywhere in a document. They consist of a *parent* and *content* property: `<!--text-->`

Table 2.1 summarizes the most important properties for all node kinds:

node kind	parent	children	attr	target	content	value	uri	name	ns
document		+					✓		
element	✓	+	+					✓	+
attribute	✓					✓		✓	
text	✓				✓				
proc.-instr.	✓			✓	✓				
comment	✓				✓				

Table 2.1: Summary of node properties (✓: fixed size, +: variable size)

It turns out that the respective properties of all node kinds exhibit a great variety. Whereas all node kinds – except document nodes – have a *parent* reference, other properties are only used by a few kinds. Consequently, a naïve tabular storage would result in many empty fields, or NULL values. Next, textual fields have variable length. Even more, some properties contain complex data types. The number of children, attributes, and namespaces per element node is variable. The *names* of elements and attributes are defined as *QName* instances, which consist of a *prefix*, a *local name*, and a *namespace URI* [FMM+07]. Similarly, namespaces have their own *prefix*, *URI* and *parent* reference.

2.3.7 Namespaces

Namespaces allow users to uniquely name and address elements and attributes in XML documents of different sources. Whereas the principal benefit of having namespaces is undisputed, there has been some discontent with the actual solution, as both users and developers are frequently confused by its intricate details and complexity[2]. In a nutshell, namespaces consist of an optional prefix and a URI. The URI serves as unique node identifier across multiple nodes and documents, whereas the prefix can be used to bind a URI to certain nodes. As a consequence, two documents can have the same prefix and still reference different URIs. New namespaces can be defined for each element, and they are valid for all descendant elements unless they are overwritten by another namespace. Prefixed names of elements or attributes are bound to the correspondent local namespace. Elements without prefix are bound to the global namespace URI, and attributes without prefix do not belong to any namespace. If the URI is empty, namespaces are undeclared and reset to their default. The flexible nature of namespaces demands additional efforts on a database storage. Some details on storing namespaces can be found in 2.4.1.1.

2.4 Pre/Dist/Size Mapping

In this section, as a result of the discussion on different mappings, the combination of *pre*, *dist*, and *size* will be presented in more detail, as it both represents a compact storage pattern and efficiently supports all XPath axes. Some normalization steps will now be proposed to minimize the memory consumption and, as a corollary, access time.

The title of this thesis might raise the question what "large XML instances" actually are [WG09]. In Computer Science, address spaces are always limited: no data structure can have infinite size. Regarding Moore's Law, the notion of size is closely intertwined with technical progress; at the time of writing, XML documents with a few megabytes were still regarded as large by many publications.

In the scope of this work, we propose a data structure that allows mapping up to 500 gigabytes of XML data to a single database instance. In practice, the actual size of an instance will usually be smaller, as additional document properties may restrict the maximum size. As will be shown in the following, the chosen limits represent a compromise between execution speed and the size of real-life documents. The address space of the presented data structure can be easily extended to meet future demands.

---

[2]see www.stylusstudio.com/xmldev/201004/post40000.html, or www.jclark.com/xml/xmlns.htm for examples

2.4. Pre/Dist/Size Mapping

2.4.1 Address Ranges

2.4.1.1 Analysis

The pre property has been presented as node identifier. A pre value is sequentially assigned to each node in the document. As a result, all pre values will be dense and sorted. The number of assigned pre values (which will be referred to as *document size* from now on) is dependent on the document structure: the larger text nodes are, the less pre values are needed. As a consequence, an address limit for pre values will be reached earlier if a document has short texts. If nodes are sequentially stored in a database, the pre value does not have to be stored at all, as it will be implicitly given by the node offset. If updates are performed, the *virtual pre* value will not cause any extra costs.

The $dist$ property represents the relative distance to the pre value of the parent node. While its value will be small for many XML nodes, it can get as large as the current pre value if a node references the root of a document. In practice, the $dist$ value gets large for all node kinds, except for attribute nodes, as elements have a relatively small number of attributes. As a consequence, a smaller address range can be reserved to store the $dist$ values for attributes. For document nodes, the $dist$ property can be discarded.

The $size$ property reflects the number of descendants. For the root node, it will equal the document size. Nodes with a small level depth (i.e., which are close to the root node) have a larger $size$ value than nodes that are deeply nested. The range of the $size$ value varies, dependent on the node kind: texts, comments, processing instructions and attributes will never have children. Accordingly, their $size$ value is always 0 and does not have to be physically stored. If only one document is stored in a database, the $size$ value of a document node equals the document size and can be discarded as well.

If attributes are *inlined* in the main database structure (see 2.4.2.1 for details), an $asize$ property can be added to map the number of attributes. As elements are the only kinds that have attributes, the property can be omitted for all other kinds. As a counterpart to the $dist$ value of attributes, $asize$ will always be small, compared to the standard $size$ value.

The id property serves as unique node identifier. While its value equals the pre value if the document is initially traversed, it will differ as soon as nodes are deleted or inserted in the database. Its maximum value corresponds to the number of document nodes, and increases with each node insertion. Consequently, a renumbering of the id values may become necessary when the limit of the address space is reached. As will be discussed in

2.4. Pre/Dist/Size Mapping

2.6, the *id* is only required if both additional, content-based index structures are created and updates need to be performed. In other words, it can be omitted if all database operations will be read-only, or if updates are performed, but no content-based index structures are needed to speed up queries.

The remaining node properties are independent from a specific XML encoding: Most textual XML content is addressed by the *text* property, which exists for text, comment, and processing instruction nodes. Attributes have a similar *value* property, which, in this context, will be treated as *text*. To further unify the representation, the *target* values of processing instructions will be merged with the text values, and the *document uri* of document nodes will as well be treated as text. A single 0 byte is used as delimiter to separate all strings from each other.

As text lengths can be highly variable, it seems appropriate to only store a pointer in the main database structure. Several solutions exist for such a reference:

1. All strings can be organized by an additional index structure. As the number of (both total and distinct) texts is always smaller than the total document size, the index reference will never exceed the maximum *pre* value, respectively its address range.

2. The indexing of complete text node imposes some overhead to the database construction process – particularly if documents are too large to fit in main memory. A straightforward alternative is to sequentially store all texts to disk. A simple directory maps the database references to text offsets.

3. While the second solution offers a clean abstraction between document structure and textual content, the directory structure occupies a considerable amount of additional space. Memory can be saved if the text offset is directly referenced from the database. The address range for textual references will have to be extended as, in most cases, the total text length will be greater than the number of *pre* values.

For disk-based storage, Solution 3 will be pursued in the following, due to its simplicity and compactness, although it is worth mentioning that the other solutions could speed up querying and be more flexible regarding updates. For instance, Solution 1 seems more appropriate for a main memory database representation, as lookup times are very fast in primary storage (see 2.5.3 for details).

Both elements and attributes have a *name* property. As name strings have variable sizes as well, all names are indexed, and a fixed-size numeric reference is used as database entry. As the number of distinct names is much smaller than the actual number of elements and attributes, a small address space suffices to store the name reference. Each element and attribute node has a unique namespace, the URI of which is also stored in an index. As documents and collections have a limited number of namespaces, all index references can be usually mapped to a small address space[3].

Namespaces, which are specified by element start tags, also result in a tree. Likewise, common namespace structures are comparatively small. As they are frequently accessed by XPath and XQuery requests, they are kept in main memory as a conventional tree structure. For each element node, an additional ns flag is added to the storage to indicate if an element introduces new namespaces.

node kind	$dist$	$size$	$asize$	id	$text$	$name$	uri	ns
document	c	+	c	+	+			
element	+	+	–	+		–	–	–
attribute	–	c	c	+	+	–	–	
text	+	c	c	+	+			
proc.-instr.	+	c	c	+	+			
comment	+	c	c	+	+			

Table 2.2: Summary of normalized node properties.
+/–: large/small address space, c: constant value

A normalized distribution of all node properties is shown in Table 2.2, along with a first and approximate estimation of the required address space. Compared to Table 2.1, the number of unused cells has been reduced, and all variable-sized entries have been externalized and replaced by numeric references. Cells with constant values need not be stored in the table, but are indicated as well.

2.4.1.2 XML Instances

To refine the optimal address range for all node properties, it is mandatory to take a look at real-world XML documents. In our context, the following document characteristics are relevant:

- the number of XML nodes (**#nodes**) is needed to determine the address space for the pre, $dist$, and $size$ property.
- the number of attributes (**#atr**) reflects the maximum number of attribute nodes

---

[3]No official rules have been specified on how XML documents should be built or designed. Outliers, however, are generally regarded as malformed or – as Michael Kay puts it – "pathological" [Kay08]

2.4. Pre/Dist/Size Mapping

of a single element node. It defines the address space for the $asize$ property, and the $dist$ property for attributes.

- the number of distinct element names (**#eln**) and attribute names (**#atn**), including namespace prefixes, serves as upper limit for the numeric $name$ reference.

- the number of distinct namespace URIs (**#uri**) defines an upper limit for the numeric uri reference.

- the total length of text nodes (**ltxt**) and attribute values (**latr**) indicates the address range for the $text$ property. For simplification, processing instructions and comments have been conflated with text nodes.

In Section 4.3, a great variety of XML instances is analyzed in detail. Table 2.3 summarizes the statistical results for the instances that yield maximum values for the focused node properties. Note that the table is meant to sound out the limits of the discussed encoding. In practice, most instances handled by our database system are much smaller:

INSTANCES	file size	#nodes	#atr	#eln	#atn	#uri	ltxt	latr
RUWIKIHIST	421 GiB	324,848,508	3	21	6	2	**411 GiB**	186 MiB
IPROCLASS	36 GiB	**1,631,218,984**	3	245	4	2	14 GiB	102 MiB
INEX2009	31 GiB	1,336,110,639	15	**28,034**	451	1	9.3 GiB	6.0 GiB
INTERPRO	14 GiB	860,304.235	5	7	15	0	19 B	**6.2 GiB**
EURLEX	4.7 GiB	167,328,039	**23**	186	46	1	2.6 GiB	236 MiB
WIKICORPUS	4.4 GiB	157,948,561	12	1,257	**2,687**	1	1.5 GiB	449 MiB
DDI	76 MiB	2,070,157	7	104	16	**21**	6 MiB	1 MiB

Table 2.3: Value ranges for XML documents and collections.
See Table 4.5 for a complete survey

As demonstrated by the RUWIKIHIST and IPROCLASS databases, a larger file size does not necessarily result in a larger number of database nodes: the large size of individual text nodes in the Wikipedia corpus leads to a relatively small node structure. Other document characteristics, such as long element and attribute names and structuring whitespaces, may as well contribute to larger file sizes without affecting the node number. The file size/nodes ratio of all tested 59 databases amounts to the average of 90 Bytes/node and a standard deviation of 229. This ratio can be used as a guideline to estimate how many nodes a database will have for an average XML document: the average maximum input document size amounts to 181 GiB.

Next, most documents have a small number of attributes per element (#atr). In our test results, the EURLEX document – a heterogeneous dataset that has been assembled from many different sources – has a maximum of 23 attributes. As a result, a small address space suffices for the *asize* property, and for the *dist* property of attribute nodes. The number of element and attribute names (#eln and #atn) is small for single documents, but may increase if multiple documents are stored in a single database. This can be observed for the INEX2009 collection, embracing around 2,7 million documents. Namespace URIs have similar characteristics: their distinct number, however, is smaller. Most documents do not specify more than two namespaces, or none at all. In our test documents, the maximum number of namespaces was encountered in the DDI document collection. Other examples for XML datasets with up to 20 namespaces are OpenDocument [Wei09] and Open Office XML [ECM06] documents.

2.4.2 Table Mapping

In Section 2.3, a distinction was made between *set-based* and *sequential* processing. From now on, we will focus on a sequential and native storage variant with the following key properties:

1. The structure of XML documents is mapped to a flat *table* representation.
2. An XML node is represented as a fixed-size *tuple* (record).
3. The tuple *order* reflects the original node order.
4. The *offset* (row number) serves as pre value.

After an analysis of the concrete bit ranges that have to be supplied, a node will be represented in a fixed number of bits, which can later be directly mapped to main memory and disk. Some optimizations will be detailed that further reduce the size of the eventual data structure and speed up querying.

2.4.2.1 Attribute Inlining

By definition, XML attributes have elements as parent nodes. Yet, attributes are not treated as ordinary child nodes, as they are owned by an element and have no fixed order. Next, the attribute names of a single element must not contain duplicates. As a consequence, attributes are stored in a different way than child nodes by many implementations, such as e.g. Natix [FHK+02] or MONETDB/XQUERY [BMR05]. An alternative approach, which has been pursued in this work, consists in treating attributes the same way as child nodes and *inline* them in the main table. A big advantage of inlining is that no additional data structure needs to be organized in order to store, query and update attributes. An additional benefit is that queries on attributes will be executed

2.4. Pre/Dist/Size Mapping

faster, as the memory and disk access patterns are simplified, leading to less random requests. A drawback may be that the *size* property cannot be utilized anymore to request the number of XPath descendants of a node, as it now comprises all attributes in the subtree. Instead, the *asize* property returns the exact number of attributes per node.

2.4.2.2 Bit Ranges

Some maximum ranges are now defined to map documents to memory areas. In Table 2.4, the value ranges from Table 2.3 are broken down to bit ranges. The #nodes column indicates that the *pre*, *dist*, *size* and *id* values of the IPROCLASS and the INEX2009 database take up to 31 bits, thus occupying the full range of a signed 32 bit integer. This means that integer pointers can be used to reference table entries. Depending on the programming language, the address range could be doubled by using unsigned integers. Next, by switching to 64 bit, the address range could be extended to a maximum of 16 exabytes. In the context of this work, we decided not to further extend the address range as, on the one hand, array handling is still optimized for 32 bit in some programming environments[4] and, on the other hand, most real-life database instances did not come close to our limits.

INSTANCES	file size	#nodes	#atr	#eln	#atn	#uri	ltxt	latr
RUWIKIHIST	421 GiB	29	2	5	3	1	39	28
IPROCLASS	36 GiB	31	2	8	2	1	34	27
INEX2009	31 GiB	31	4	15	9	1	34	33
INTERPRO	14 GiB	30	3	3	4	0	5	33
EURLEX	4.7 GiB	28	5	8	6	1	32	28
WIKICORPUS	4.4 GiB	28	4	11	12	1	31	29
DDI	76 MiB	21	3	7	4	5	23	21

Table 2.4: Bits needed to allocate value ranges

The maximum length for texts and attribute values, as shown in the #ltxt and #latr column, defines the limit for the *text* property, and takes 39 bits. Element and attributes names are referenced by the *name* property and are limited to 15 and 12 bits, as indicated by #eln and #atn, respectively. The *asize* and the *uri* properties occupy a maximum of 5 bits (see #atr and #uri).

---

[4]See e.g. http://bugs.sun.com/view_bug.do?bug_id=4963452 for details on current limitations of pointer handling in Java. In short, array pointers are limited to 31 bit (signed integers) in Java. This limit would enforce additional pointer indirections if all table data is kept in main memory, and slow down processing. It does not lead to restrictions, however, if the table is stored on disk.

2.4.2.3 Compactification

Table 2.5 is an updated version of Table 2.2. It contains concrete bit range limits for all node properties. Two columns have been added: the *kind* property adds 3 additional bits, which are needed to reference the six different node kinds. The #bits column adds up the bit ranges. It summarizes how many bits are needed to map all properties of a specific node kind to memory. The *ns* property, which is only defined for elements, indicates if namespaces are defined for the respective element. As such, it needs a single bit.

node kind	*kind*	*dist*	*size*	*asize*	*id*	*text*	*name*	*uri*	*ns*	#bits
document	3	0	31	0	31	40				105
element	3	31	31	5	31		16	8	1	126
attribute	3	5	0	0	31	40	16			95
text	3	31	0	0	31	40				105
proc.-instr.	3	31	0	0	31	40				105
comment	3	31	0	0	31	40				105

Table 2.5: Concrete bit ranges for all node kinds

As can be derived from the resulting compilation, the element node demands most memory. While the optional *asize* property could be discarded, all other properties are mandatory for processing. In spite of their name/value combination, attribute nodes take up the least number of bits, as they have no children and a small distance to their parent node. All other node kinds occupy the same bit range in our representation, as their textual properties have been merged in the *text* property.

The #bits column suggests that a single element node can be represented within 16 bytes. As 16 is a power of 2, it represents a convenient size for storing entries in fixed-size memory, such as blocks on disk. To map other node kinds to the same bit range, an individual bit distribution was defined for each node kind. The three *kind* bits serve as indicator where the value of a specific property is placed. An exemplary bit distribution, which has been applied in Version 6 of our database system, is shown in Figure 2.3.

2.4.2.4 Integer Inlining

Values of text and attribute nodes may belong to specific data types that can be specified by a schema language, such as DTD or XML Schema. Whereas some database systems opt to store texts dependent on their type (such as PTDOM [WK06]), most systems choose a schema-oblivious approach, as the complexity of schema languages and the

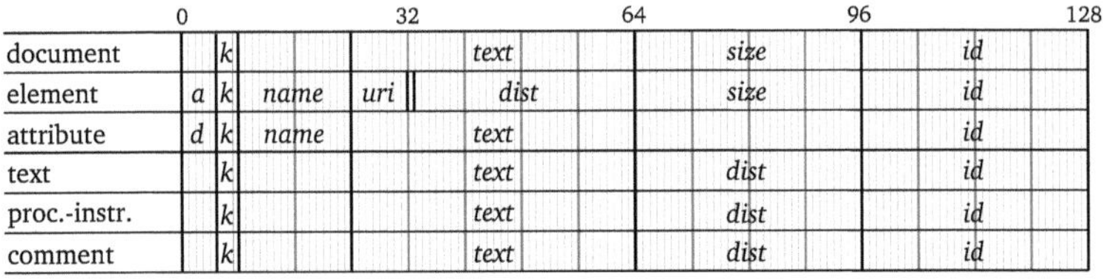

2.4. Pre/Dist/Size Mapping

	0					32		64		96		128
document		k				text		size			id	
element	a	k	name	uri		dist		size			id	
attribute	d	k	name			text					id	
text		k				text				dist	id	
proc.-instr.		k				text				dist	id	
comment		k				text				dist	id	

Figure 2.3: Bitwise distribution of node properties in BASEX 6.0.
Note: the ns bit is located to the right of the uri property

flexible structure of documents complicate a type-aware implementation. It is one key feature of XML that no schema needs to be defined at all – and, at the same time, a drawback, as relational database systems can benefit from the fact that data types are known in advance. In our architecture, by default, texts are stored as UTF8 strings, suffixed by a 0 byte and linked by a reference from the main table, which means that, for instance, a single integer value may take up to 16 instead of 4 bytes in the storage[5].

A different storage strategy can be applied for data types that can be dynamically recognized by analyzing the incoming data. Integer values are the easiest ones to detect: if a string comprises up to 10 digits, it can be *inlined*, i.e., treated as a number and stored in the main table instead of the textual reference. In our representation, up to 11 bytes can be saved for each integer. The uppermost bit of the reference can be used as a flag to state if the *text* value is to be treated as pointer or actual value. This way, no extra lookup is necessary to determine the type. If all contents of a document are numeric, no additional text structures will be created at all. A positive side effect of inlining is that even strings that were not supposed to be handled as integers can be stored more economically.

The inlining technique could be extended to various other data types. In the scope of this work, it was limited to integers in order to minimize the parsing effort while building databases and requesting textual data. Next, to comply with the first encoding requirement that has been specified in 2.3, we need to guarantee that the original document is exactly reconstructed. This means that no normalization steps may be performed on the input data, such as stripping whitespaces, or removing upper and lower case. As a consequence, strings such as "true", " true ", and "TRUE" cannot be simplified and

---

[5]5 bytes are needed for the reference, up to 10 bytes for the string representation of an integer ($2^{32} = 4294967296$), and an additional byte for the null byte suffix.

treated as the same boolean value.

2.4.2.5 Updates

A wide range of numbering schemes have been discussed to support updates in XML documents [CKM02, SCCS09]. ORDPATH [OOP+04] is the most popular *prefix labeling scheme* that has been derived from the Dewey Order [TVB+02]. The document order and hierarchy is preserved by the labeling scheme, and new nodes can be added and deleted without relabeling the existing nodes. As hierarchic labels have variable length and can get very memory consuming for deeply nested nodes, ORDPATH labels are additionally compressed and represented as bit strings. Although the proposed scheme has experienced numerous tweaks and variations to save space [AS08, AS09] and to cover navigational and locking issues [HHMW07], it can still be considered as rather bulky: all labels have to be organized by at least one additional index structure.

As the basic *pre/size/dist* encoding has primarily been designed with the objective of minimizing the storage overhead and the number of data structures, it needs to be extended as well to support efficient updates. A naïve attempt to delete a node from the main table demonstrates that the current architecture is insufficient. Let n be the *pre* value of the node to be deleted and $size(db)$ the total number of database nodes[6]:

1. all tuples in the range $[n + size(n), size(db)]$ need to be moved by $-size(n)$
2. $size(n)$ needs to be subtracted from the $size$ value of all ancestors of n

While the second operation is cheap, as only a number of $height(n-1)$ tuples have to be touched, the first operation yields high physical costs, and a worst case $O(size(db))$ if updates occur at the beginning of the document.

A classical solution to circumvent the problem is the introduction of logical pages. Several tuples are mapped to blocks with fixed size, and a flat directory is added that contains the first *pre* values (*fpre*) and references to all pages (*page*). This way, tuple shifts can be limited to the affected blocks. All tuples are contiguously stored from the beginning of the page to avoid additional lookup operations for free and used page entries. The number of tuples of a page p is calculated by subtracting the current from the subsequent *fpre* value: $fpre(p+1) - fpre(p)$.

---

[6] Note that insert operations lead to similar costs.

2.4. Pre/Dist/Size Mapping

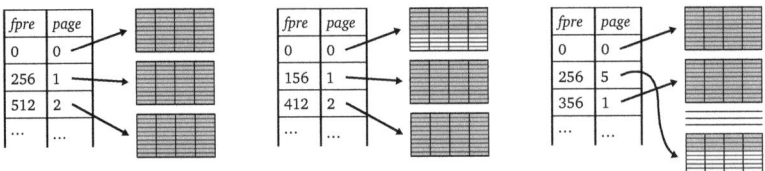

Figure 2.4: Directory of logical pages: a) initial state for a page size of 4096 bytes, b) deletion of 100 nodes, and c) insertion of 100 nodes

Figure 2.4 illustrates an exemplary directory, for which the size of a logical page was set to 4096 bytes, in compliance with the size of a typical disk page. As one tuple occupies 16 bytes, a maximum of 256 tuples is stored per page. In 2.4 b), a node n has been deleted; its 99 descendants ($size(n) = 100$) have all been located in the first page p. After the deletion and the update of all $size$ values of the ancestors of node n, $size(n)$ is subtracted from all subsequent entries $p+1$ in the directory. Example 2.4 c) shows the mapping after an insert operation: 100 nodes are inserted at $pre = 256$, resulting in the creation of a new page (here: 5) at the end of the existing pages and the insertion of a new entry in the directory.

Even for large databases, the directory will stay comparatively small, so that it can be usually kept in main memory. Let P be the number of tuples per page, which is the page size divided by the tuple size, and $max(db)$ the maximum database size. If n values need to be stored per dictionary entry, a total of $\frac{n \cdot max(db)}{P}$ values needs to be handled, yielding $2 \cdot 2^{31}/(4096/16) = 16777216$ integers and a memory consumption of 64 MiB in our representation. Although the deletion and insertion of dictionary entries requires copying large main memory areas, the operation is cheap, compared to update operations on disk. If even larger pre ranges are to be supported, or if update performance proves to be too inefficient for large database instances, the dictionary structure can be extended to a conventional B-Tree and stored on disk [BM72].

MONETDB/XQUERY, which is based on the $pre/size/level$ encoding, offers a similar solution by adding a new $pos/size/level$ table to the storage, which is divided into logical pages [BMR05]. The original table serves as a view on the new table with all pages in order. A new $node$ property resembles the id property in our representation and serves as unique node identifier. As attributes are stored in extra tables, an additional table maps $node$ to pos values. Pages may contain gaps to improve page locking behavior for the update of ancestor nodes. – A different solution has been chosen in our context, as the presented directory is very light-weight and does not require extra tables. Next, the *dist* property, which is absent in MONETDB/XQUERY, allows constant access to parent nodes, which makes updates on ancestors a very cheap operation. An id/pre mapping (the equivalent to $node/pos$) can be omitted as well, as attributes are *inlined* in the main table. Last but not least, the directory can initially be omitted, and created on-the-fly as soon as the first update operation is performed. Consequently, there is no need to explicitly differentiate between read-only and updatable databases.

2.5 Database Architecture

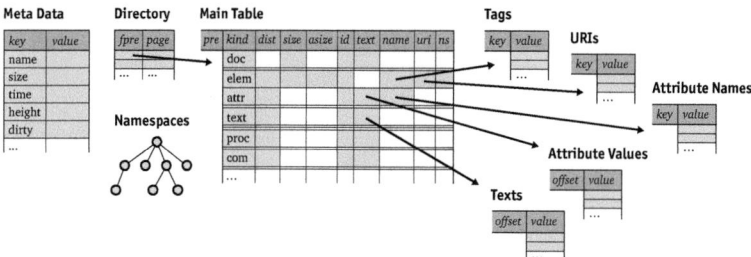

Figure 2.5: Main structure of a database instance

Figure 2.5 summarizes the last paragraphs and shows the overall structure of a single database instance. *Virtual* columns, which are not explicitly stored, are indicated only by their header. The main table contains numeric keys to the tags, namespace URIs, and attribute name indexes. Texts (incl. processing instructions, comments, and URIs of document nodes) and attribute values are stored in extra files or arrays, the offsets of which are referenced from the main table. The directory contains pointers to the first pre value of each table page. Various information is supplied as meta data, such as the name of the database, its size, modified time, tree height, or dirtiness after updates. A main memory tree, which is backed by additional prefix/URI indexes, provides access to namespaces.

2.5.1 Database Construction

The tabular representation of XML can be constructed in linear time. An event-driven SAX parser [MB04] is applied to build a database instance. While pre and $post$ (and most

2.5. Database Architecture

other) values can be sequentially stored in the table in a single run[7], the $size$ value has to be subsequently updated as soon as the number of descendants of the correspondent node is known.

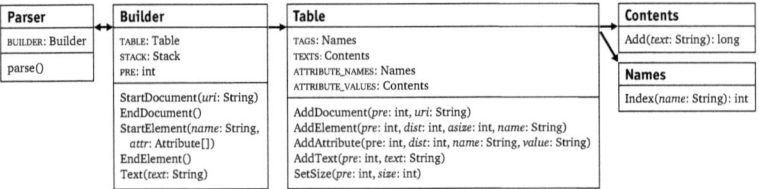

Figure 2.6: Class diagram for building a database with a SAX parser

Figure 2.6 depicts the most relevant classes for building a database via SAX. A new PARSER instance is created by the central BUILDER instance, which in turn notifies the builder of XML events to be processed. A global PRE value serves as counter for new nodes to be stored in the table, and a STACK is used to cache the pre values of current ancestor nodes. Processed node values are passed on to the TABLE instance, which passes on textual values to the CONTENTS and NAMES objects. We will now have a closer look on the most important SAX events; for the sake of simplicity, advanced issues such as namespaces and common implementation details for SAX parsers will be omitted, and database creation will be restricted to a single document.

Algorithm 2 Builder.StartDocument(uri: String)
---
1   initialize TABLE and STACK
2   PRE := 0
3   TABLE.AddDocument(PRE, uri)
4   STACK.Push(PRE)
5   PRE := PRE + 1

Algorithm 2 is called by the parser when the document is opened: The global TABLE and STACK instances are initialized, the PRE counter is set to 0, and the document tuple $\{pre/text\}$ is added to the table. Next, PRE is pushed to the stack and incremented by one.

In Algorithm 3, the distance to the parent node ($dist$) is calculated by subtracting the pre value of the last parent node, located on top of the stack, from the current PRE counter.

---
[7]SAX algorithms for the $pre/post$ encoding are found in [Gru02]

2.5. Database Architecture

Algorithm 3 Builder.StartElement(*name*: String, *attr*: Attribute[])
1   $dist := $ PRE $-$ STACK.peek()
2   $asize := \#attr + 1$
3   TABLE.AddElement(PRE, $dist, asize, name$)
4   STACK.Push(PRE)
5   PRE $:= $ PRE $+ 1$
6   **for** $a := 0$ **to** $\#attr - 1$ **do**
7     $dist := a + 1$
8   TABLE.AddAttribute(PRE, $dist, attr[a].name, attr[a].value$)
9   PRE $:= $ PRE $+ 1$
10 **end for**

$asize$ is set to the number of attributes, and 1 is added so that $pre + asize$ will point to the first node behind the attribute list. The resulting $\{pre/dist/asize/name\}$ tuple is added to the table and, once again, PRE is pushed to the stack and incremented. Next, all attribute tuples $\{pre/dist/name/text\}$ are added. The $dist$ value equals the current offset counter added by 1.

Algorithm 4 Builder.EndElement()
1   $size := $ PRE $-$ STACK.pop()
2   TABLE.SetSize(PRE, $size$)

If an element is closed, as shown in Algorithm 4, the most recent stack value (which is the pre value of the corresponding opening element) is popped. The difference between the PRE counter and the stack value is the $size$ value, and is stored in the table.

Algorithm 5 for storing text nodes is even simpler: a tuple $pre/text$ is added to the table, and the PRE counter is incremented. The events for processing instructions and comments are nearly identical.

Algorithm 5 Builder.Text(*text*: String)
1   TABLE.AddText(PRE, $text$)
2   PRE $:= $ PRE $+ 1$

Finally, in Algorithm 6, the document node is closed, and the $size$ value of the root node is updated. – Note that subsequent tables updates might slow down a sequential disk storage. As a straightforward optimization, the $size$ values can be cached and written to the database in a second run.

Before a tuple can be stored, strings need to be dissolved into references and stored in

2.5. Database Architecture

Algorithm 6 Builder.EndDocument()
1 $size := \text{PRE} - \text{STACK.pop}()$
2 TABLE.SetSize(PRE, $size$)

extra data structures. Algorithm 7 demonstrates this process for attributes: the *name* of the attribute is indexed, and its key is stored in the main table.

Algorithm 7 Table.AddAttribute(*pre*: int, *dist*: int, *name*: String, *value*: String)
1 $attn := \text{ATTRIBUTE\_NAMES}.\text{Index}(name)$
2 $attv := \text{ATTRIBUTE\_VALUES}.\text{Add}(value)$
3 add attribute tuple $\{pre, dist, attn, attv\}$ to storage

As detailed in Section 2.4.2.4 and shown in Algorithm 8, the file or array offset is used as reference for *text* values. If the value is numeric, it is converted to its numeric representation and flagged with a number bit (here: NUMBERMASK), which is the highest bit of the selected bit range.

Algorithm 8 Contents.Add(*text*: String): long
1 $v := $ convert *text* to integer
2 **if** v is valid **then**
3      $v := v \mid \text{NUMBERMASK}$
4 **else**
5   add *text* to storage
6      $v := $ offset to stored *text*
7 **end if**
8 **return** v

2.5.2 Generic Parsing

The presented database construction process is limited to single XML documents. In order to process multiple files and directories, the Builder and Table algorithms can be extended to add the *dist* values of document nodes to the storage, and to perform the initialization of the global variables before the first call of Algorithm 2.

To go further, we can observe that XML is just one possible textual representation of tree hierarchies: a multitude of other representations have been proposed, such as JSON [Cro06] or OGDL [Vee09]. Even more, arbitrary tree structures can be converted to XML. The presented SAX interface allows all kinds of sources to be used as input for the database builder. While, by default, one or more XML documents are sent to and

2.5. Database Architecture

processed in the existing architecture, the existing parser can be defined as abstract and extended by a range of specific implementations. Some examples for parsers (or *importers*), which have been realized in our project, are listed in the following:

- Most filesystems exhibit a hierarchic structure, which can be mapped to XML in a straightforward manner. A filesystem parser recursively traverses all directories and triggers events to add directory and file elements to the database. The idea has been pursued in the DeepFS project [HGS09].

- MAB2 is a flat, textual exchange format for German library meta data [Bib99], which can be converted to XML. The resulting tree structure facilitates an easier access to hierarchic relations for multi-part volumes and series. An importer for MAB2 data has been added for the MEDIOVIS project [GGJ$^+$05].

- HTML is a markup language that has been inspired by SGML. As the majority of real-life HTML documents are malformed, they usually cannot be read by XML parsers. Instead, converters like TagSoup [Cow08] can be applied on the input as a pre-processing step to create a well-formed XML document, which can then be processed by the actual XML parser.

- the CSV format can be used to store tables as plain text. One line of text contains a single record, and all fields are separated by commas. An importer for CSV files consists of a few lines of code, as tables can be easily represented as a tree structure.

2.5.3 Main Memory vs Persistent Storage

External storage is known to be slower than main memory by some orders of magnitude. In practice, the distinction is often not perceived by end users anymore, as much of the data, which has been read at least once, is automatically remembered in disk and main memory caches, the size of which has steadily increased over the last years. The difference shrinks even more with the popularization of solid state disks, which have much better random access times. At the same time, the available main memory in today's personal computers has reached a size which is, for many use cases, large enough to hold complete database instances.

An obvious advantage of mapping databases to main memory is that the execution time for queries can be further minimized. While the buffer management of the operating system generically speeds up access to frequently requested data, a main memory database

2.5. Database Architecture

system offers even better performance as the access patterns are known in advance. If XML documents are to be processed on-the-fly, they need not be stored on disk at all. However, the time needed for mapping existing databases to main memory may invalidate the performance lead for single queries. Next, main memory allows no persistent storage; updated data gets lost if it is not eventually backed up on disk.

The proposed database structure was designed to be both mappable to primary and secondary storage. While completely identical storage patterns could have been chosen, the existing database builder was split up in order to exploit beneficial properties of the respective target:

- in the disk-based variant, all tuples are distributed into blocks. To improve platform independence, storage and partitioning of the resulting blocks is completely left to the disk manager. Additionally, all texts and attribute values are sequentially written to disk, and their offsets are referenced from the main table.

- in main memory, tuples are organized in flat byte arrays, which are continuously resized to accommodate new tuples. Texts and attribute values are indexed, and the resulting keys are referenced in the main table. To guarantee that the value indexes contain all contents of a database, numeric texts will not be inlined in the table, but instead be indexed as well (see also 2.4.1.1).

As a consequence, all database operations, including those which perform updates and access index structures, can be performed on both the main memory and the external storage variant. Figure 2.7 shows the extended architecture for constructing databases, including the generic parser interface; performance results on the two representations are given in Section 4.2.2.2.

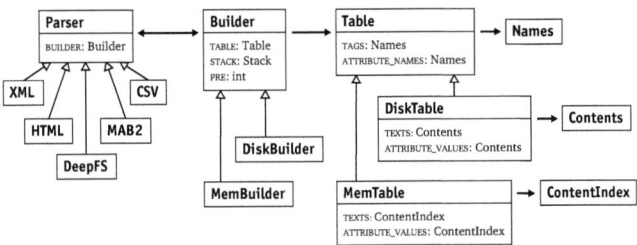

Figure 2.7: Class diagram: extended architecture for database construction

2.6 Index Structures

In short, databases indexes exist to speed up query evaluation. In relational databases, usual index structures are value indexes, and column-based, i.e., applied on one or more attributes, of a table. In XML, due to the complexity of tree structures, a wide range of index structures exists, for which different classifications can be found in the literature [MWA+98, CMV05]. In the scope of this work, we will focus on the following three index types:

1. *Name* indexes organize frequently occurring strings, such as tag or attribute names, in small main memory structures.

2. *Path*, or *structural* indexes facilitate the access to all unique document paths of a document. Path indexes have initially been proposed for object-oriented and nested relational databases [BK89].

3. *Value* or *content* indexes are comparable to index structures of relational databases. Texts and attribute values of documents are indexed for faster access. Full-text indexes are a specialized type of value indexes.

2.6.1 Names

Repeating tag and attribute names are the main reason why XML has become notorious for its verbosity. In XML databases, the most straightforward approach to reduce space is to introduce a name index, which replaces variable-size names by numeric ids (see [JAKC+02] or [Mei02] for examples). This can be done by storing all names in a main memory based associative array, such as a hash or binary search tree. In the scope of this work, separate indexes are created for elements and attributes. As shown in Section 2.4.2.2, 16 bits, or *short* values, suffice to reference single names in a document.

Name indexes could be enhanced with the pre/id values of all corresponding elements or attributes. This approach would allow a direct lookup of all descendant nodes that use a specific tag or attribute name, as e.g. needed for the simple XPath query //name. Due to the substantial space overhead of such an index and additional maintenance operations necessary for each update, we discarded the storage of pre values in an early stage. Instead, statistical meta information on nodes were added to the name indexes, which can later be utilized by the query compiler to choose between different execution plans:

2.6. Index Structures

- A *counter* property states how often a name occurs in the database.
- A *leaf* flag indicates if an element is a leaf node, i.e., if it has no more elements as descendants.
- A *length* property stores the maximum length of the associated child text or attribute value.
- A *kind* property reflects if the associated values are numbers, string categories, or strings.
- min and max values contain the lower and upper limits of numeric values.

Algorithm 9 Name.UpdateStatistics(String value)

Require:
    MAXCATS := number of maximum allowed categories
    initialize CATEGORIES, KIND := INTEGER, MIN := ∞, MAX := $-\infty$ before first call
1   **if** KIND $\neq$ STRING and #CATEGORIES $<$ MAXCATS **then**
2   add $value$ to CATEGORIES
3   **end if**
4   **if** KIND = INTEGER **then**
5   v := convert $value$ to integer
6   **if** v is valid **then**
7   **if** MIN $> v$ **then** MIN := v **end if**
8   **if** MAX $< v$ **then** MAX := v **end if**
9   **else**
10   KIND := CATEGORY
11   **end if**
12   **end if**
13   **if** KIND = CATEGORY **then**
14   **if** #CATEGORIES = MAXCATS **then**
15   KIND := STRING
16   **end if**
17   **end if**

All information can be iteratively collected while a database is created. Algorithm 9 demonstrates how string categories and the min, max, and $kind$ values are generated for a single element or attribute. The function is initialized with the strictest precondition, which assumes that all values are integers in the empty range $(\infty, -\infty)$. As soon as the first value arrives, it will be added to CATEGORIES, an array that stores a limited number of distinct strings. Next, as the current $kind$ is INTEGER, the value is converted to an integer. If the conversion is successful, min and max will be set to this new value. If more integers are found in subsequent calls, min and max will be updated each time.

2.6. Index Structures

If an incoming string is no integer, CATEGORY will be set as new *kind*. If more distinct strings have been collected than are allowed by the MAXCATS constant, the *kind* is set to the most general STRING kind. In the last case, no more checks will be performed on the remaining strings.

If updates are performed, the statistics lose their accuracy, but continue to serve as guideline for the query compiler. As an example, $kind$ =INTEGER, $min = 1$, and $max = 2$ for the c attribute in the following document:

```
<A><B c="1"/><B c="2"/><B c="2"/></A>
```

The query compiler can speed up query evaluation by replacing a subquery @c<1 with the static boolean value `false`, as the comparison will never be true for the given document. If the node <B c="1"/> is deleted in a next step, the new actual minimum for attribute c will be 2. The index statistics will not be updated, however, as the complete database – or at least all nodes that use the name in question – would have to be scanned in order to calculate the new lower limit. Instead, the given subquery will be rewritten the same way as before, while the subquery @c<2 will be evaluated in full, and still yield correct results, as no attribute will be found that fulfills the test. If new nodes are inserted, or if existing nodes are modified in the database, the same methods as for creating a new database can be used to update the existing meta information.

More details on exploiting the index information during query compilation can be found in 3.3.1.5.

2.6.2 Path Summary

While the *name* index collects atomic information on tag and attribute names of the same name – no matter where they occur in a document – a *path summary* organizes all distinct element and attribute paths that occur in a document or database. Path summaries are also called path indexes or structural summaries [RM01, CMS02]. They are all derived from the DataGuide [GW97], a data structure that has first been applied in the LORE system [MAG+97], which has been introduced in 2.2.

If schema information is predefined by a DTD or XML Schema, it can be used to build a path summary for a given document. A predefined (*static*) schema can reduce the implementation effort:

- The actual input does not need to be parsed to build the summary.

2.6. Index Structures

- If update queries will only be processed if their results comply with the given schema, the path summary needs not be updated at all.

Dynamic schemas, however, which are built from the actual input, have some advantages as well:

- Many static, real-life schemas are bulky and contain paths that are not actually used by a document. As a consequence, dynamic schemas will be more accurate for a specific document/database.
- As a document needs to be parsed anyway if a new database is created, the path summary can be built in the same run and enriched with additional, input specific meta information.

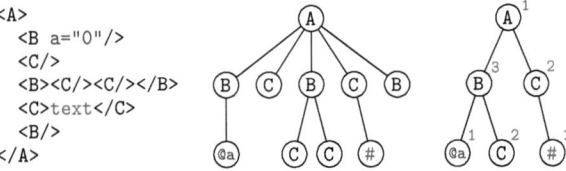

Figure 2.8: XML document, tree representation, path summary incl. cardinalities

Figure 2.8 depicts a path summary for a simple XML document. As a summary is usually very small, compared to the original document, it is represented as a main memory tree structure. Similar to the name index, nodes of a path summary could be enriched with references to the XML nodes that match the location paths. Again, this approach was discarded in our architecture to minimize the overhead for storing and updating the database. To further reduce memory consumption, the path nodes reference the keys of the existing tag and attribute name index.

The path summary is useful in numerous applications. In the visual frontend of our database, which will not be further detailed in this work, path completions can be suggested while XQuery expressions are typed in by the user. Next, the summary is queried by the Scatterplot, Table and Explorer view to verify how many nodes exist in the tree hierarchy, or if certain nodes have descendants. Section 3.3.1.5 will demonstrate how the summary is used by the query compiler.

2.6. Index Structures

2.6.3 Values

In the relational world, classical index structures are *value* (or *content*) indexes, which facilitate content-based queries in sub-linear time. Most value indexes rely on standard tree or hash structures with *key* and *value* pairs. As the use and construction of these indexes are well-known concepts, we will focus on features that are specific to XML and the discussed storage. Values in this context are strings from texts or attribute values.

Different variants of value indexes can be found in existing XML databases [GGHS09b]:

- Keys can be indexed on *document level*, an approach which is usually taken by relational engines. Queries on many small documents may be accelerated by this approach, whereas there is no benefit for single and large documents.

- Certain *location paths* can be pre-selected for being indexed. While this approach seems promising at first glance, and might reduce the size of the index structures, it often fails when queries are nested or getting more complex. Moreover, indexes must be manually added, and database users need explicit knowledge on the available index structures.

- Implementation-specific *XQuery functions* can be added to directly access the index structures. Again, knowledge on database internals is required, and a compiler will not be able to benefit from the indexes, as the user alone chooses whether the index is to be used.

To support a wider range of optimizations, we decided to index all text nodes by default, regardless of their position in the document structure. In Section 3.3.2, the query optimizer is presented. It will rewrite and invert location paths and predicates whenever an index access is possible and (potentially) cheaper than a conventional query execution. Due to our tabular encoding, sorted lists of pre values – which are identical to id values as long as no updates are performed – will be used as pointers to the main table. As the index structure, which will be discussed in the following, has been optimized for performance and low memory consumption, update operations are not supported. Instead, the following optimizations will be applied to reduce the index size to a minimum:

1. pre values will be compressed before they are stored in the index.
2. Instead of the absolute values, distances between pre values will be stored.
3. As common user queries contain short keywords – compared to the maximum length of text nodes in a document – the index size can be reduced by ignoring all strings that exceed a specified maximum length.

2.6. Index Structures

4. The variable-length keys need not be stored in the index at all; instead, they can be looked up in the main table by following the first referenced *pre* value.

2.6.3.1 Compression

A fast and simple compression mechanism, inspired by the UTF-8 encoding, is applied to all *pre* values in the index structure. As summarized in Table 2.6, the first two bits of a byte are used to define the range of the next integer to be parsed. Depending on the bit code, a single integer will occupy 1-5 bytes in its compressed representation: small integers will take less space, whereas large integers will occupy one additional byte.

Encoding (binary)	Range (hex)		Description
00bbbbbb	00 -	3F	1 byte maps 2^6 values
01bbbbbb B	40 -	3FFF	2 bytes map 2^{14} values
10bbbbbb B B B	4000 -	3FFFFFFF	4 bytes map 2^{30} values
11000000 B B B B	40000000 -	FFFFFFFF	5 bytes map 2^{32} values

Table 2.6: Compression of numeric values. b represents a bit, B represents a byte

If the second optimization of 2.6.3 is applied, which suggests to replace absolute values by distances, the total index size will further shrink, as distances are much smaller than absolute values and thus can be better compressed.

2.6.3.2 Construction

A quick insight is given on how the value index is constructed for either texts or attribute values: The main table is sequentially scanned. If a node with the addressed kind is encountered, and if the length of the string to be indexed does not exceed the maximum, predefined length, the string and current *pre* value are passed on to the index builder. The values are added to a main memory, balanced binary tree. After all nodes were scanned, the binary tree is traversed in preorder, and the index data is stored to disk in two files, or entities:

- a *values* file contains all variable-size lists with compressed *pre* distances.
- a *keys* file contains a simple array with offsets to the *pre* lists.

As the binary tree has been processed in preorder, all stored offsets will be sorted by the lexicographical order of their keys. This means that binary search can be applied by index requests to find the *pre* values for a given string in logarithmic time. As the actual strings (keys) are not stored in the index themselves, they are looked up by following the offset to the current *pre* list and accessing the main table via the first *pre* value.

2.6.3.3 Main Memory Awareness

Although the presented index builder was designed to be conservative in terms of memory consumption, it will eventually hit main memory limits if the processed documents get too large. In general, 20-30% of the size of the documents needs to be provided as main memory to guarantee a successful index construction. Depending on the characteristics of the input, either keys or values may be responsible for memory overflows. If many identical strings are found (i.e., if few *categories* exist, as introduced in Section 2.6.1), most space will be consumed for the *pre* value lists. If the document contents are rather heterogeneous, the keys are likely to dominate memory consumption.

To support for even larger inputs, the existing index builder can be rewritten to take the available amount of main memory into consideration. The resulting approach is loosely inspired by classical algorithms, such as External Sort [Knu73] or Sort-Based Inversion [WMB99]. It supports all kinds of document types and, yet, is fast and straightforward: As soon as the available main memory is exhausted, the current tree structure is written to disk, and a new, empty tree is created, which stores new keys and values. After all nodes have been processed, the temporarily written index structures are merged into one single tree. The merge can be performed in a single run as, thanks to the sequential construction process, all *pre* values in the intermediate index files are sorted. This way, the index size will only be limited by the free disk space, no matter how much main memory is left. If enough memory is available, there will be no need to write temporary index instances to disk at all.

2.6.4 Full-Texts

While value indexes have been a classical feature of relational databases, full-text indexes have originally been developed for Information Retrieval applications. Today, all major relational database systems include implementation specific extensions to query textual corpora. In XML, however, the XQuery Full Text (XQFT) language extension was developed to offer a standardized and unified way for accessing and retrieving full-texts [AYBB[+]09] (see 3.1.3 for more).

Full-text indexes are applied to speed up queries on single words of documents. Before texts can be indexed, they need to be *tokenized*, i.e., split into atomic units (tokens),

2.6. Index Structures

which serve as keys for future index requests. The tokenization process might include various language dependent normalization steps, all of which are also defined in XQFT:

- Case sensitivity (lower and upper case) is removed.
- Diacritics (umlauts, accents, etc.) are removed.
- Tokens are stemmed via algorithms or dictionaries.
- A thesaurus may be applied on the tokens.
- Eventually, tokens are skipped that are defined in an optional stop word list.

The resulting dictionary, which contains all tokens of a document, will usually have much less keys than values, as the number of distinct words is limited for most text corpora[8]. Values will occupy much more space, as single words are contained in several text nodes, and even contained several times in single nodes. The token positions within a text node will be denoted by the *pos* property: they are stored as well to efficiently support advanced XQFT features such as phrase, distance or window queries.

Full-text queries can be performed on arbitrary inputs, such as attribute values or dynamically generated strings. In this section, we will focus on the index construction of text nodes, as this is the most frequent use case in practice (note that the XQFT implementation, which is detailed in Section 3.1.3, supports queries on arbitrary inputs). The following document is derived from Gath's master thesis [Gat09]. It will serve as input for the upcoming index structures:

```
<PAGE>
  <TITLE>Fuzzy String Searching!</TITLE>
  <TEXT>Fuzzy string search is the name that is used for a category of techniques
    for string searching/finding strings that approximately match some given pattern
    string (approximate or inexact matching).</TEXT>
</PAGE>
```

After removing case and some stop words, the tokenization process yields the following terms (token positions *pos* are shown in superscript):

```
<PAGE>
  <TITLE>fuzzy⁰ string¹ searching²</TITLE>
  <TEXT>fuzzy⁰ string¹ search² name⁵ used⁸ category¹¹ techniques¹³
    string¹⁵ searching¹⁶ finding¹⁷ strings¹⁸ approximately²⁰ match²¹ pattern²⁴
```

---

[8]Exceptions are input that are not based on natural language, such as genome sequences. Texts corpora of this kind are dependent on specialized tokenizers, as linguistic normalization steps will lead to useless tokens and dictionaries.

string[25] approximate[26] inexact[27] matching[28]</TEXT>
</PAGE>

In the following, two full-text index structures will be outlined, which have been developed in the scope of this work: while the first one is centered on specialized approximate matches, and the second one supports wildcard queries, both versions yield very fast results for exact queries. Again, the presented index structures are read-only, as the clear focus was set on performance, memory consumption, and full scalability.

2.6.4.1 Fuzzy Index

id	key (i)	values (pre/pos)	length $|i|$	id
0	name	5/5	4	0
1	used	5/6	5	2
2	fuzzy	3/0, 5/0	6	4
3	match	5/21	7	6
4	search	5/2	8	10
5	string	3/1, 5/1, 5/15, 5/25	9	12
6	finding	5/16	10	13
7	inexact	5/27	11	14
8	pattern	5/24	13	15
9	strings	5/18		
10	category	5/11		
11	matching	5/28		
12	searching	3/2, 5/16		
13	techniques	5/13		
14	approximate	5/26		
15	approximately	5/20		

Table 2.7: Fuzzy Index instance, sorted by token length and lexicographical order

The main memory predecessor of the fuzzy index was a structure named FUZZEARCH. It was developed in the course of the MEDIOVIS project [GGJ+05] to query approximate user search terms in a library catalog in sub-linear time. In this index structure, all index terms $w \in W$ are sorted first by their token length $|w|$ and second by their lexicographic order. A second table references the first id for each token length. For exact searches on term t, it suffices to perform a binary search on all index terms that have the same length as the input term (i.e., $|t| = |w|$). For approximate searches, an optimized variant [Ukk85] of the Damerau-Levenshtein edit distance [Dam64, Lev66] is applied on the index terms as follows: let $k > 0$ be the maximum number of errors allowed. All index terms with length from this range $[|t| - k; |t| + k]$ may be possible hits, which means that terms with $|w| < |t| - k$ or $|w| > |t| + k$ need not be considered as potential results. In

2.6. Index Structures

usual scenarios, a small value is chosen for k (e.g., $\lfloor |t| \div 4 \rfloor$) to ignore terms that differ too much from the original string.

Table 2.7 shows the index for the given XML sample. If the search term $t=$"fuzz" is specified in a query, and if one error is allowed ($|t| = 4$, $\lfloor |t| \div 4 \rfloor = 1$), it is sufficient to calculate the edit distance for all terms w with $|w| \in [3; 5]$, which are all terms with $id \in \{0, ..., 5\}$. The index term "fuzzy" will be accepted as a hit, and two pre/pos combinations $\{3/0, 5/0\}$ will be returned as results.

2.6.4.2 Trie Index

The Patricia trie [Mor68], a compressed tree structure derived from the classical trie [Fre60], is a well-established data structure for building string dictionaries. Tries have linear costs, regarding the length of the search term. In addition to the fuzzy index, they also support queries with wildcards. As a drawback, however, the flexible structure of tries leads to a noticeable memory overhead.

id	key substring	children (id/first character)	values (pre/pos)
0		1:a, 3:c, 4:f, 7:i, 8:m, 10:n, 11:p, 12:s, 17:t, 18:u	
1	approximate	2:1	5/26
2	ly		5/20
3	category		5/11
4	f	5:i,6:u	
5	inding		5/16
6	uzzy		3/0, 5/0
7	inexact		5/27
8	match	9:i	5/21
9	ing		5/28
10	name		5/5
11	pattern		5/24
12	s	13:e,15:t	
13	earch	14	5/2
14	ing		3/2, 5/16
15	tring	16:t	3/1, 5/1, 5/15, 5/25
16	s		5/18
17	techniques		5/13
18	used		5/6

Table 2.8: Trie Index instance, tabular representation

In the presented index structure, memory consumption is reduced by compressing pre and pos values, as was done for the value index (see 2.6.3.1). Next, as motivated e.g. in [AMS92], the trie structure is flattened and stored in arrays. Similar to the storage of XML documents, trie nodes are mapped to a flat table, thus reducing pointer handling to

2.6. Index Structures

a minimum. A table entry contains the respective key substring, links to all child nodes and the first letters of their substrings, and pre/pos value combinations. By caching the first letters, the next child node can be found without traversing all other child entries.

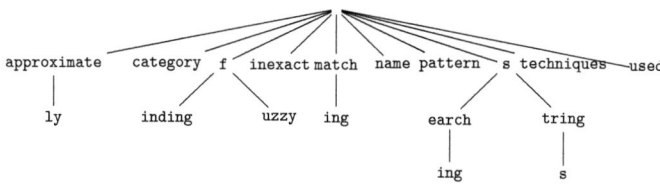

Figure 2.9: Trie representation of the XML sample document

Figure 2.9 depicts the trie mapping for the XML sample, which is represented in tabular form in Table 2.8. To find all results for the wildcard pattern "search.*", the table entries 0, 12, 13, and 14 need to be touched. The last two entries match the search pattern and thus yield the pre/pos combinations $\{3/2, 5/2, 5/16\}$.

3 Querying

3.1 XML Languages

Every storage architecture, no matter how lightweight or powerful, requires an interface for accessing its data. By introducing SEQUEL (a "structured English query language" [CB74]) for relational data, Chamberlin and Boyce acknowledged early that a unified query language may help both users to communicate with database systems[1]. With the advent of tree data, new languages were proposed to do justice to the upcoming challenges. Resulting from a number of attempts, which were based on SQL and OQL, XML-QL was the first language that focused on XML [DFF+98]. Element patterns could be defined to match data in documents. The following sample query prints all authors from books published by BooxX, which are found in a library.xml document:

```
WHERE <book>
        <publisher>BooxX</publisher>
        <author>$a</author>
      </book>
IN "library.xml"
CONSTRUCT $a
```

Next, XQL was proposed [RLS98]. As summarized in Table 3.1, one or more XML documents are now defined as input, and the document's tree structure is the data model which is mapped by a query. To represent hierarchical relationships, the child (/) and descendant (//) operators were added to the language. A filter operator [...] could be appended to further refine the result. By specifying numbers in the filter, results were filtered by their context position.

---

[1] The notion of what "users" actually are is a popular subject for discussion, and it has changed over the years. Today, much more people have profound computer knowledge than forty years ago. At the same time, user interfaces have advanced a lot, which means that most end-users will hardly come into contact with low-level interfaces anymore. As for SQL, it has become the most popular language for developers and programmers to interact with relational databases.

43

3.1. XML Languages

SQL	XQL
The database is a set of tables.	The database is a set of one or more XML documents.
Queries are done in SQL, a query language that uses the structure of tables as a basic model.	Queries are done in XQL, a query language that uses the structure of XML documents as a basic model.
The `FROM` clause determines the tables which are examined by the query.	A query is given a list of input nodes from one or more documents.
The result of a query is a table containing a set of rows; this table may serve as the basis for further queries.	The result of a query is a list of XML document nodes, which may serve as the basis for further queries.

Table 3.1: Comparison between SQL and XQL (taken from [RLS98])

The following subsections are supposed to give a brief overview on the languages XPath and XQuery, that resulted from XML-QL and XQL, and their Full Text and Update extensions. XSLT will not be part of this survey. Its expressiveness is similar to XQuery [Kay04], and it has been shown that XSLT expressions can be compiled into XQuery [FRSV05]. It is primarily used for transforming smaller XML fragments into other formats, and not for querying large XML instances, which is the focus of this chapter.

3.1.1 XPath

Due to its status as W3C Recommendation [CD99], and due to its simplicity, XPath 1.0 has become the *de facto* standard for traversing XML documents. It serves as a subset for other languages, namely XQuery and XSLT. The most important XPath expression in our context is the *location path*, which is composed by one or more *location steps* separated by slashes. A single step consists of three components:

- the *axis* specifies the tree relationship between the incoming and resulting nodes,
- the *node test* defines the node type or name of a resulting node, and
- optional *predicates* further refine the result set.

A location step consumes an incoming node set (which might initially be a single document node) and generates a new node set by traversing the specified axis and filtering the resulting nodes by the node test and predicates. Thirteen *axes* are defined in XPath:

- *Forward axes* contain nodes that occur after the initial node in document order: *child*, *attribute*, *descendant*, *descendant-or-self*, *following*, and *following-sibling* belong to this category.
- *Reverse axes* yield nodes before the initial node: these are *parent*, *ancestor*, *ancestor-or-self*, *preceding*, and *preceding-sibling*.

3.1. XML Languages

- The *self* axis returns the original node, and the *namespace* axis (obsolete since XPath 2.0) returns namespaces.

Axis and node tests are separated by two colons. A *node test* filters nodes by their type:

- `node()` accepts all nodes,
- `text()`, `comment()`, `processing-instruction()` accepts the respective type,
- a *QName* (which consists of an optional namespace prefix and a local name) filters attributes and elements by their name, and
- an asterisk (*) serves as wildcard for all attribute and element names.

Predicates are arbitrary expressions enclosed by brackets [...]. If the boolean result of an expression yields true, a node is accepted. If the result is numeric, a predicate is called *positional*: a node will be accepted if the current context position equals this number. For instance, if the predicate evaluates to the integer 3, all nodes except for the third will be discarded.

An abbreviated syntax improves the legibility of XPath expressions. The most prominent abbreviations are the following:

- `attribute::` can be represented by the *at* sign @.
- `child::` can be omitted as child is the default axis.
- a period . is equivalent to `self::node()`.
- two periods .. are equivalent to `parent::node()`.
- `/descendant-or-self::node()/` can be written as two slashes //.

Contrary to XQL, the two slashes frequently lead to misunderstandings, as they are often mixed up with the descendant axis: as `//node()` contains an additional abbreviated child step, it can be rewritten to `/descendant::node()`. In contrast, the location path `//self:node()` is the same as `/descendant-or-self::node()` (see also 3.3.1.5).

XPath offers additional expressions, such as boolean connectives, comparison operators, calculation expressions, or simple functions. A location path can be introduced by an arbitrary expression, e.g., by a function for opening a document. In XPath 2.0, expressions can occur anywhere inside a path.

The XML-QL example from the beginning of this chapter can be written in XPath as compact and simple as follows:

```
doc("library.xml")//book[publisher = "BooxX"]/author
```

3.1. XML Languages

3.1.2 XQuery

XQuery is a direct successor of the Quilt query language [CRF00]. It was not until 2007 that Version 1.0 was finalized as W3C Recommendation [BCF+07]. Due to its versatility, XQuery is increasingly called "Information Processing Language" [ABF+09]. It offers many more features than a pure query language, and it poses more challenges to a query optimizer, as will be discussed later:

- With XQuery, new contents and XML fragments can be generated. In contrast, XPath or SQL is typically used to extract contents from existing resources.
- An arbitrary number of documents and collections can be accessed by a single query. Names of documents to be queried can be generated at runtime.
- Similar to object-oriented languages, functions and modules can be defined in XQuery to make complex queries more readable and reusable.
- As the input data to be processed might not be known in advance, XQuery 3.0 introduces *nondeterministic* functions, which do not always return the same result.

The following definitions will be used throughout this chapter: A single XQuery has a *root expression*, which may have an arbitrary number of sub-expressions. Each expression evaluates to a *value*. All values are flat *sequences*, i.e., ordered collections of zero or more items. An *item* has a fixed data type, which is either an *atomic value* (string, integer, etc.) or a *node* (element, attribute, text, etc.).

Apart from some exceptions, XQuery is regarded as a functional language. As such, functions do not have side-effects, and variables are immutable once they are assigned. The iterative FLWOR expression can be used to bind intermediate values to variables, and to formulate nested, join-like queries. As higher-order functions are an important feature of functional languages, XQuery 3.0 will also allow functions to be passed on as arguments.

Again, the XML-QL example is rewritten to XQuery, using a FLWOR iterator. As XPath is a subset of the language, the XPath expression shown before is valid XQuery as well:

```
for    $book in doc("library.xml")//book
where  $book/publisher = "BooxX"
return $book/author
```

In contrast to SQL, XQuery has no explicit database logic: two functions doc($string) and collection($string) are provided to address resources. As the specified string

3.1. XML Languages

argument may point to any resource, such as a remote file, or a local file or directory, it depends on the implementation if resources will always be looked up in a database or dynamically retrieved from the specified URI. In the scope of this work, we pursue a hybrid approach: a database is opened if a database instance exists for the given URI. Otherwise, a temporary database instance is created for the original file. This way, both databases and XML documents can be accessed by a single query.

More details are found in the official language specification [BCF+07]. In the next sections, this document will serve as standard reference for XQuery.

3.1.3 XQuery Full Text

In the introduction of this thesis, it has been indicated that many XML documents are document-centric [BBB00], i.e., contain large semi-structured texts. As such, full-text capability is needed to perform content-based queries. While, at the time of writing, many implementations offer their own retrieval extensions, the official W3C XQuery Full Text 1.0 Recommendation (XQFT, to be finalized in 2010 or 2011) will serve as a new standard for bringing the XML and Information Retrieval world closer together.

XQuery contains some basic functions to find substrings. The evaluation of a full-text expression is a much more elaborated process: The incoming query and input strings are *tokenized*, i.e., split into atomic units (*tokens*), and then compared one by one. As detailed in 2.6.4, the tokenization process can include several operations, which are dependent on the natural language of the input, such as the removal of case sensitivity or diacritics, or stemming. Differences between a simple substring search and tokenization are supposed to be illustrated by two examples:

- XQuery: `contains("ab", "a")` → true
  XQFT: `"ab" contains text "a"` → false
- XQuery: `contains("Träume", "traum")` → false
  XQFT: `"Träume" contains text "traum"`
     `using stemming using language "de"` → true

The `contains text` keyword pair introduces a *full-text selection* in XQFT. The left and the right side of the expression can contain arbitrary sub-expressions. For the Mondial document[2], this query will yield true:

---
[2]Source: `http://www.cs.washington.edu/research/xmldatasets/www/repository.html`

3.1. XML Languages

```
"This text contains country names, such as Japan and Korea."
  contains text { doc("mondial-3.0.xml")//country/name }
```

Along with the boolean query result, an implementation-defined score value is calculated, which allows an ordering of the results by relevance. The order clause of a FLWOR iterator can be used to sort score values. In the following query, all country names will be sorted according to a score value that is calculated by the full-text expression:

```
let $doc := doc("mondial-3.0.xml")
for $p score $s in $doc//country[religions contains text "Catholic"]
order by $s descending
return <hit score="{ $s }">{ $p/name/text() }</hit>
```

XQFT boasts numerous optional operators, filters and options to allow users to specify a full-text search as concisely as possible:

- Logical connectives `ftor`, `ftand`, `ftnot`, and `not in` (mild not) can be used to combine several tokens.

- Using the `weight` keyword, individual weights can be attached to single tokens.

- The way how containment is checked can be specified by `any`, `all`, or `phrase`. As an example, `all words` demands that all words of a token sequence are found in the input.

- The `occurs` keyword indicates cardinality selections, which determine how often a token needs to occur in the input.

- Match options, introduced by the `using` keyword, influence how the tokenizer works. Possible options are `stemming`, `case sensitive`, `wildcards`, and others.

- An additional `language` match option can be used to perform tokenization for the specified language.

- Positional filters specify the distance between single tokens. Tokens can be constrained to appear `ordered`, in a specified `window`, within a given `distance`, or in a certain scope (`sentence` or `paragraph`).

Our BASEX query processor was the first – and, at the time of writing, is still one of the few – to fully support the XQuery Full Text Recommendation [AYBB$^+$09][3]. All optional

---

[3] An XPath/XQuery Test Suite is offered by the W3C to test the conformance of an implementation. All implementations, for which test results have been submitted, are listed at this link: http://dev.w3.org/2007/xpath-full-text-10-test-suite/PublicPagesStagingArea/ReportedResults/XQFTTSReportSimple.html

3.1. XML Languages

features have been implemented as well, except for the *ignore option*. Among developers, the upcoming XQFT Recommendation is being met with mixed reactions. While some appreciate its complexity, others criticize precisely this property. As the specification opens the way to arbitrarily combine and nest all available options, the resulting queries may get difficult or even impossible to optimize, particularly if the expressions are meant to be processed by an optional full-text index. Some XML databases, such as EXIST or SEDNA, circumvent this dilemma by offering simple XQuery full-text functions. In this work, we decided to choose the rocky path by supporting the full range of XQFT features, and optimizing all kinds of queries to access available index structures as often as possible.

General insight on query rewriting for index access is given in 3.3.2, and performance results are presented in 4.2.3. For detailed information on the intricacies of XQFT, the reader is referred to Gath's master thesis [Gat09].

3.1.4 XQuery Update

While full-text functionality may be regarded as an optional feature – at least for users coming from the relational corner – update capability is a core requirement of each database language. The first intent to standardize updates in XML was XUpdate [LM03], in which updating expressions were represented in XML itself. With the following snippet, a phone element is inserted after the name element of an address:

```
<xupdate:modifications version="1.0"
       xmlns:xupdate="http://www.xmldb.org/xupdate">
  <xupdate:insert-after select="//address[@id = 1]/name" >
      <xupdate:element name="phone">+1-22-334455</xupdate:element>
  </xupdate:insert-before>
</xupdate:modifications>
```

The rather verbose syntax was adopted by early XML database systems and is now gradually replaced by the upcoming W3C XQuery Update Facility (XQUF), which allows for a more concise syntax and is more complete. The above query can be represented in a single-line expression:

```
insert node <phone>+1-22-334455</phone> after //address[@id = 1]/name
```

With XQUF, nodes can be deleted and inserted, existing nodes can be updated without their node identity being changed, and existing nodes can be copied to intermediate instances, and modified. A query is defined as one snapshot: all update expressions

49

that occur in a query are not immediately processed, but instead collected in a *pending update list*, which is executed only at the end of the query execution. While this solution seems unfamiliar at first glance, it helps to simplify error handling and to minimize side effects, which are caused by the heterogeneity of XML documents.

Another advantage is that pre values, which may occur as intermediate references to other database nodes, need not be changed during query execution. As has been shown in 2.4.2.5, deletions and insertions only affect database nodes n with $n \geq pre$. As a consequence, before updates are carried out, all operations are sorted by the pre value of the target nodes. All updates are then applied in a backward manner: the operation with the largest pre value is executed first, followed by the remaining operations with decreasing pre values. This way, all used pre values will remain valid until the end of query execution.

Implementation details and performance results on XQUF are beyond the scope of this work and can be looked up in Kircher's bachelor thesis [Kir10].

3.2 Query Processing

A raw XPath or XQuery is represented as a simple string, and classical compiler techniques are needed to convert the input into executable code. As literature on compilation construction offers a broad terminology for classifying the necessary transformation steps, we will base our wording on the XQuery Recommendation, which divides query processing into the two phases: *Static Analysis* and *Dynamic Evaluation* [BCF+07]. As an extension, the first phase was split up into two transformation steps, namely *analysis* and *compilation*. The second phase is represented by the *evaluation* and *serialization* step.

3.2.1 Analysis

Before a query can be executed, the input is interpreted and transformed into an executable data structure. The process of splitting the incoming byte stream into atomic *tokens* is called *lexical analysis*. In the subsequent *syntax analysis* step, an *expression tree* is built from the tokens, using a formal *grammar*. The grammar of XQuery and other XML Recommendations is based on the EBNF notation [Wir77] and can be parsed by an

3.2. Query Processing

LL(1) parser[4] in a rather straightforward manner.

The division into lexical and syntax analysis can help to keep the resulting code more readable. The complexity of XQuery, however, requires a lexical scanner to have knowledge on its current *lexical state*, as e.g. detailed in a W3C working draft on parsing XPath and XQuery [Boa05]. The following list demonstrates that a simple token "for" can have different semantics, as it might occur in a:

- FLWOR expression: `for $i in 1 to 10 return $i`
- text node: `<xml>marked for delivery</xml>`
- comment: `(: needed for result output :)`
- node constructor: `element for { "text" }`
- variable: `declare variable $for := 1;`
- location path: `/xml/for/sub`
- string: `"for all of us"`

To avoid the distinction between too many different lexical states, which all lead to different scanning branches, it is common to merge the two steps and scan and convert the input by a single parser. While existing analyzers and parser generators, such as FLEX, BISON, or JAVACC, could have been used to convert the XQuery grammar to an executable parser, we decided to write our own parser to get better performance – an approach that has also been taken by other query processors, such as SAXON or QIZX. The parser performs the following steps:

- The *static context* is initialized. It contains global information on the query, such as default namespaces, variables, functions, or statically known documents.
- The input is analyzed and converted to expressions, all of which form the *expression tree* (synonymous: *query plan*).
- Parse errors are raised if the input does not comply with the LL1 grammar and extra-grammatical constraints.
- As a function may call another function that has not yet been declared in a query, all function calls need to be verified after the whole query has been parsed.

Figure 3.1 depicts some of the expressions that are created by the parsing step, or will be computed by the evaluation step. All expressions are derived from the abstract *Expression* class. A *Value* is either an *Item* or *Sequence*. Items of type *Node* may either

---

[4]LL(1) means: Left to right, Leftmost derivation, one look-ahead

3.2. Query Processing

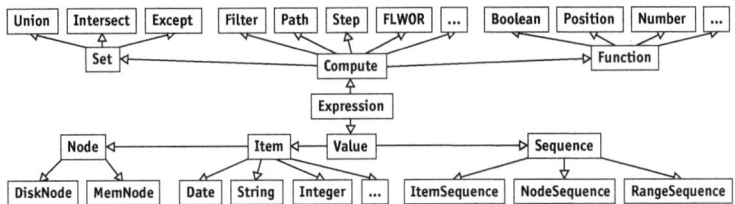

Figure 3.1: Class diagram with expression types

refer to a database node or a main-memory fragment, created by a node constructor. Sequences are further subdivided into *ItemSequence, NodeSequence,* and *RangeSequence* types, which offer optimizations for items of a specific type. All other expressions, such as *Set* and its subtypes, *Filter*, etc. are derived from the *Compute* expression.

3.2.2 Compilation

Formal Semantics were defined for XQuery 1.0 [DFF+07] as an intent to standardize the normalization of queries, including the atomization of effective boolean values, or static typing. Due to the complexity of the language and its subtleties, this effort was discontinued with Version 3.0. All implementations may choose their own compilation steps as long as the query results conform to the specification.

Compilation includes all steps that simplify and optimize the expression tree (details will be discussed in 3.3):

- Static operations will be pre-evaluated.
- Expressions will be rewritten if their arguments always yield `true` or `false`.
- FLWOR expressions and location paths will be simplified.
- Predicates will be rewritten to access available index structures.
- Unknown tags or attributes will be removed.
- Static type checks will be performed before the query is evaluated.

3.2.3 Evaluation

In the evaluation step, the resulting item sequence of an expression is computed. For simple and static queries, all necessary computation steps might have been performed in the optimization step, and the root expression to be evaluated might already contain the final result. For more complex expressions and queries that rely on dynamic input, such as XML documents or fragments, most of the total time for processing will be taken by the evaluation step.

3.2.4 Serialization

After the expression has been computed, the serializer transforms the result into a readable, textual format. The process of serializing the query result has been formalized as well in another W3C Recommendation [BKT$^+$07], which defines a set of parameters to control the textual representation. However, the serialization interface is not mandatory for a XQuery implementation: In many scenarios, it is recommendable to pass on and process a result in its object representation.

In a processing pipeline, iterative query evaluation will speed up evaluation in many cases, as large intermediate results can be avoided. If an XQuery expression is processed in an iterative manner, query results will be discarded as soon as they have been processed. Accordingly, if the results are passed on to a serializer, the evaluation and serialization step will be closely intertwined, as each resulting item will be directly serialized and discarded after serialization. Details on the iterative processing model are found in 3.4.1.

3.3 Optimizations

In spite of the complexity of the language, more than fifty XQuery processors are available by now[5]. While a high conformance with the specification is an important indicator for the quality of an implementation[6], the speed of an implementation might be even more relevant for users, particularly if large XML documents are to be processed.

Query optimization is an established area of research in the database community (see [Ioa96] for an overview), and it seems obvious that many existing techniques can be adapted and applied to XML as well. This has already been proven by a number of other implementations: Once more, LORE was the first XML system to integrate both

---

[5]An list of all implementations is found on the W3C XQuery homepage: `http://www.w3.org/XML/Query`
[6]The XQuery Test Suite with around 15,000 queries is used to test the conformance of an implementation: `http://dev.w3.org/2006/xquery-test-suite/PublicPagesStagingArea/XQTSReportSimple.html`. As of August 2010, only SAXON reaches 100% of the test suite, followed by BASEX with 9 failed tests.

3.3. Optimizations

logical and physical query optimization [MW99]. Query rewritings for the BIZQUERY system were presented in [GK02] and served as input for SEDNA. Other optimizations were discussed for the BEA [FHK+04] and SAXON [Kay08] XQuery processors. The wide variety of optimization proposals illustrates that many optimizations depend on concrete implementation issues. As an example, reverse axis steps are expensive in a streaming environment, but need constant time if a reference to the parent node is available. Another example is the construction of fragments, which is regarded to be an expensive operation for many implementations, but is relatively cheap if main memory representations are built.

In this section, we present the most important optimizations that have been integrated in our query processor. As XQuery is not just a query language, many optimization concepts have rather been inspired by classical compiler construction than database theory. Even more, the classical division into logical and physical query optimization has been completely dropped: query rewriting and database- and cost-related optimizations have been merged into one step to benefit from database specific meta data (such as statistics or the availability of indexes) at an early stage. Subsequently, optimizations will be discussed that are performed just-in-time during evaluation. A summary on the most important XQuery expressions along with their optimizations is found in the last section of this chapter.

Before going into detail, we would like to emphasize that user feedback from the Open Source community around BASEX has played an essential role in making the system efficient and flexible enough for a wide variety of use cases and workloads. Whereas some optimization approaches have been theoretically appealing while developing the compiler, they have turned out to be rather irrelevant in practice.

3.3.1 Static Optimizations

3.3.1.1 Constant Folding/Propagation

Many sub-expressions in a query are values, or have values as arguments. As such, they will always evaluate to the same result and can be pre-evaluated once at compile time. To unfold the full potential, this process, which is known as *constant folding*, needs to be recursively evaluated on all expressions of the query tree. A complete recursive traversal of the expression tree is required for many other compilation steps; otherwise, optimizations will only be locally performed, or aborted for the arguments of an expression

3.3. Optimizations

that does not support a particular optimization. Algorithm 10 is called by the compiler. It is very simple and demonstrates how constant folding works: First, the method is recursively called for all arguments, and the resulting expression is assigned as new argument. Next, all arguments are checked for their type. If all arguments are values, the expression is pre-evaluated, and the resulting value is returned. Otherwise, the existing expression is returned.

Algorithm 10 Expression.Fold() : Expression
1   **for** a **in** ARGUMENTS **do**
2       $a = a$.Fold()
3   **end for**
4   **if** all ARGUMENTS are *values* **then**
5   **return** Evaluate()
6   **else**
7   **return** this
8   **end if**

On the right, the query plan for the query 1+2*3 is shown. First, 2*3 will be pre-evaluated. The resulting value 6 will be added with 1, yielding 7. As a result, the final value was computed before the actual evaluation is started.

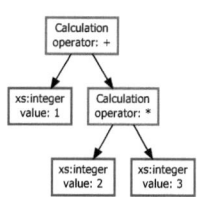

If constant folding is applied to functions as well, such as the doc() and collection() function in XQuery, static document references will be resolved and computed at compile time. This way, meta information and statistics on touched databases will be available to subsequent optimization steps.

Constant propagation is a technique related to folding: whenever a variable turns out to have a constant value, it can be statically bound to all its references in the query. Recognition of static variables is a straightforward operation in most functional languages, as all global variables are immutable and thus constant.

Some XQuery expressions, such as value comparisons, return an empty sequence if one of the arguments yields an empty sequence, and implementations are free to choose if the remaining arguments are ignored or evaluated. Algorithm 10 can be easily extended for all expressions of this kind to return an empty sequence whenever one of the arguments is empty.

3.3. Optimizations

3.3.1.2 Variable/Function Inlining

Variable expressions can also be bound to their references if they have not yet been evaluated to values. In XQuery, variables and functions without arguments are mostly similar, except that variables cannot be recursively called. Consequently, functions without function calls and arguments can be treated equally to variables. If variable and functions calls are replaced by their declarations (i.e., *inlined*), the resulting code may be subject to further local optimizations. For example, a conditional expression may be pre-evaluated to eliminate a sub-expression that will never be called. One more singularity of XQuery needs to be observed, though: node constructors generate XML fragments with unique *ids*. If a variable declaration contains a node constructor, the resulting nodes will have different node ids if they are evaluated several times:

```
declare variable $n := <xml/>; $n is $n → true
<xml/> is <xml/> → false
```

To guarantee that queries such as the first one return true, global variables will always be pre-evaluated before they are inlined.

In FLWOR expressions, variables will be dynamically assigned during runtime. While the resulting items of LET will be bound to the associated variable as sequence once, FOR iterates over the sequence, binding the items one by one. Hence, LET variables are immutable within their scope and can be treated similar to global variables – as long as they are *independent*, which means that they must not depend on other dynamic variables in the same scope. If variable references are replaced by their expressions, other variables can get independent, which are substituted next. If static typing indicates that a FOR variable will return a single item (see 3.3.1.4), it can be treated the same as LET.

The query plan shown below depicts the following query:

```
let $a := 5 let $b := $a * $a return $b
```

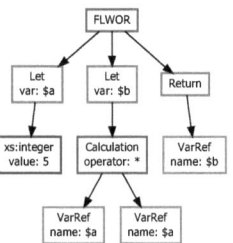

Five steps are performed to simplify the query:

- The integer value 5 is statically bound to $a.
- All subsequent variable references for $a are substituted by its value.
- Calculation 5 * 5 is pre-evaluated.
- The result 25 is statically bound to the (now) independent variable $b.

3.3. Optimizations

- The $b reference is substituted by its value.
- FLWOR is substituted by its return value 25.

Function inlining is a complex issue on its own, especially when it comes to recursive functions. For the time being, all functions can be inlined in our implementation that have values as arguments and hence can be pre-evaluated. For further studies on recursive inlining, helpful information is found in [PMC02] and [GL04].

3.3.1.3 Dead Code Elimination

After the expression tree has been simplified and rewritten, there may remain subexpressions that will have no effect on the query results, or are not accessed at all. *Eliminating* sub-trees will reduce the tree size and – even more important – reduce evaluation time by avoiding the execution of irrelevant operations.

As shown in the previous paragraphs, inlining will make variable declarations within FLWOR expressions obsolete, and the subsequent removal of all declarations in questions will speed up execution, as the repeated process of binding values to variables can be skipped. If no declarations are left, the complete FLWOR expression is replaced by the RETURN expression. If WHERE has been specified, the return value is wrapped by an IF expression.

In conditional expressions, such as if/then/else, branches can be discarded if they are known to be never accessed. If the main condition yields true, the else branch can be eliminated, and vice versa. If both branches yield the same result – which can happen after numerous simplifications of the original code – the condition itself need not be executed.

Figure 3.2 shows a query plan for another expression that can be completely evaluated at compile time. It includes a function declaration, global and local variables, and an IF expression:

```
declare function local:a() { 10 + 30 };
declare variable $b := 20 - local:a() div 10;
let $c := $b * 5
let $d := if($c > 60) then $c - 60 else $c
return $d * (20 div local:a())
```

The single optimization steps, which are dumped by the compiler, are as follows:

57

3.3. Optimizations

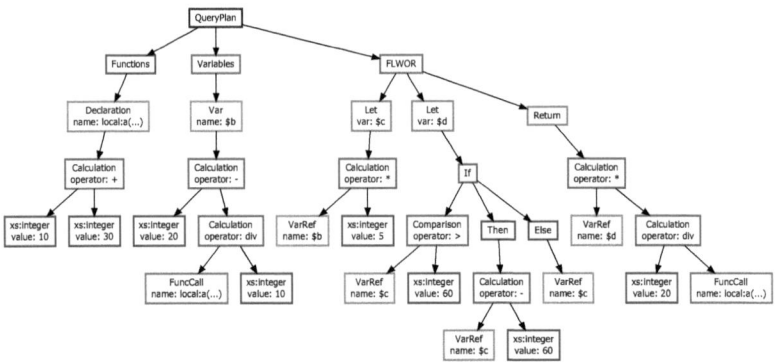

Figure 3.2: Query with a function declaration, variables, arithmetic expressions, and a conditional branch

1. pre-evaluating 10 + 30
2. inlining function local:a(...)
3. pre-evaluating 40 div 10
4. pre-evaluating 20 − 4
5. pre-evaluating 16 ∗ 5
6. binding static variable $c
7. pre-evaluating 80 > 60
8. pre-evaluating 80 − 60
9. pre-evaluating
   if(true()) then 80 − 60 else $c
10. binding static variable $d
11. inlining function local:a(...)
12. pre-evaluating 20 div 40
13. pre-evaluating 20 ∗ 0.5
14. removing variable $c
15. removing variable $d
16. simplifying flwor
17. result: `xs:integer(10)`

A second conditional expression in XQuery is `typeswitch`, which evaluates the type of its input and selects one of several expressions as result. To pre-evaluate this expression, the types of the returned values must be known at compile time – which can be realized via *static typing*.

3.3.1.4 Static Typing

XQuery is a strongly typed language, embracing a total 23 of primitive types (strings, booleans, integers, etc.; see Figure 3.3). Along with the type, a value is further specified by its *sequence type*, which also includes the cardinality (number of returned items). Values can also be *untyped*: if no XML schema is given for a specific document, all incoming strings will be of type `xs:untypedAtomic`. If an untyped value is to be processed by an expression, it will be dynamically cast to the required type. As an example, arithmetic operators convert untyped values to `xs:double` (whereas typed values will be processed without additional cast), and a dynamic error is raised if the cast fails.

3.3. Optimizations

To reduce the number of checks for runtime errors, static typing can be used to validate beforehand if an operation will always be successful, and to reduce the number of runtime checks. If both types of the arithmetic operators are numeric, they can always be added, subtracted, etc., whereas values of type xs:string and xs:integer will always result in a type error. Next, as this operator returns an empty sequence if one of the operands is empty, the expression can be pre-evaluated and substituted by an empty sequence if at least one operand has a cardinality of zero.

If values contain more than one item, the common super type is stored as a sequence type. As a result, the exact types of single items needs to be interpreted at runtime. In the filter expression (1,"a")[.], the sequence is of

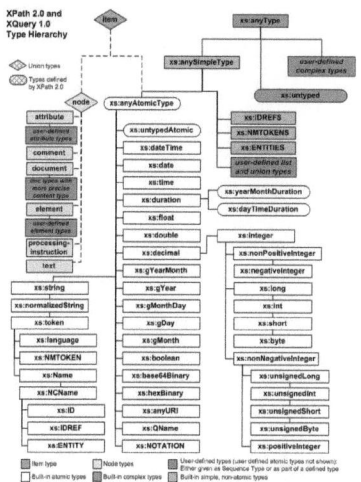

Figure 3.3: Type hierarchy of the XML Data Model [FMM+07]

type item()+. The first sequence item will cause a numeric predicate test, followed by a boolean test for the string. In contrast, if all sequence items are known to be numeric, the expression can be optimized in advance to skip the runtime test and always perform a positional test.

The existence of static types is beneficial in a number of other cases: path expressions that are composed of certain types will never yield results and need not be evaluated at all. As an example, the query //@*/node() will always return an empty sequence, as attributes cannot have child nodes. Next, the root node of a path expression must always yield nodes to be correctly evaluated.

3.3.1.5 Location Path Rewritings

As supplement to static typing, and surrogate for schema information, the path summary facilitates the validation of location paths (see 2.6.2 for a reminder). If the root of a path expression points to an existing database, or if the root context can be evaluated at compile time, as shown in 3.3.2.1, the path summary of the referenced document can be used to match the document paths against the query. If a query path is not found in

3.3. Optimizations

the summary, it can be eliminated and replaced by an empty result. If the path is too complex to be compared, or contains references to the dynamic query context, the name indexes (presented in 2.6.1) are accessed to check if single tag and attribute names occur in the database.

Moreover, the summary can be applied to speed up a path expression. In most implementations, the *descendant* step is expensive, as all descendants of the root node need to be touched, either recursively or in a linear run. If the expression is replaced by multiple *child* steps, the number of touched nodes is reduced to the distinct node paths. Four different cases may occur if a path expression //ELEM is to be optimized:

1. If the summary contains one single node with the element name ELEM, the path to this node is transformed into a location path with multiple *child* steps.

2. If several nodes exist with ELEM as element name, and if all nodes are located on the same level (i.e., if all node paths have the same length), the paths are used as input for a single location path. The paths are analyzed level by level: if the element names of all paths on a level are equal, a *child* step with this element name is generated. Otherwise, a wildcard * is used as node test to match all elements.

3. If occurrences of ELEM are found on different levels, all distinct paths will be returned and combined with a union expression.

4. If the element name ELEM is unknown, an empty sequence is returned.

Figure 3.4 includes an XML document, its tree representation and path summary. For each of the four cases, an example query is given. The fifth query was added to indicate that the example can be iteratively applied to several descendant steps.

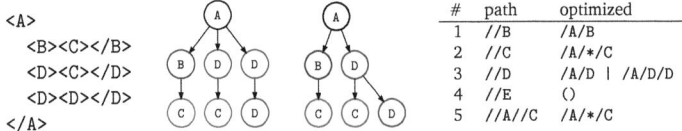

Figure 3.4: XML document, tree representation, summary, and path expressions

Path rewriting can also be applied if a location path is further refined by predicates. For example, the following two expressions are equivalent for the given document:

$$//A[1]//C[\text{text}() \text{ or } \text{comment}()] \equiv /A[1]/*/C[\text{text}() \text{ or } \text{comment}()]$$

3.3. Optimizations

In the introduction to XPath (Section 3.1.1), the two slashes (//) were introduced as an abbreviation for the construct /descendant-or-self::node()/. This construct is very expensive, as all nodes of a document are selected and, in most cases, reduced to a much smaller number of results in the subsequent location step. A simple, but very efficient optimization is to rewrite a *descendant-or-self* and *child* step to a single *descendant* step. The following queries are equivalent, but the second version is much cheaper, as the intermediate materialization of all nodes is avoided:

   //x = /descendant-or-self::node()/child::x ≡ /descendant::x

An expression with predicates can be rewritten as well, as long as they are not positional. Positions always refer to the last location step:

   //x[1] ≢ /descendant::x[1]

The original query will select each first child element of all addressed nodes, whereas the second expression will only return the first descendant element of the document. If the location path is enclosed by parentheses, the query can safely be rewritten:

   (//x)[1] ≡ (/descendant::x)[1]

Another optimization worth mentioning can be applied to the *descendant-or-self* and *attribute* steps. As only element nodes can have attributes, the node() test of the first step is rewritten to an element test (*):

   //@x ≡ /descendant-or-self::*/attribute::x

3.3.1.6 FLWOR expressions

In XQuery, numerous other equivalences exist, a fact which makes the language very flexible. For instance, many queries can be written as either pure XPath, using location paths, or XQuery, using the iterative FLWOR expression. The latter is more verbose, but some consider it to be more easily readable, particularly if queries get more complex:

```
for    $item in doc('xmark')/descendant::item
where  $item/payment = 'Creditcard'
return $item
```

The following XPath expression will yield the same result:

   doc('xmark')/descendant::item[payment = 'Creditcard']

Some FLWOR queries exist that cannot be expressed in XPath. As an example, no XPath equivalent exists for the ORDER clause, which sorts iterated values. Next, XQuery is needed to post-process items one by one, as shown in this example:

3.3. Optimizations

```
for $n in 1 to 10 return $n * 2
```

To avoid that query optimizations have to be implemented twice, both variants are first normalized to one common representation. The existing XPath representation appears to be most appropriate in our scope, as the predicate tests are already part of the expressions that might be suitable for index rewritings. Accordingly, FLWOR queries are normalized by rewriting the optional WHERE clause to one or more predicates and attaching them to the expressions defined by the variable declarations. Before the clause can be rewritten, two preconditions must be met:

1. All FOR clauses must not specify a positional or a full-text scoring variable.

2. A recursive algorithm checks if all occurrences of the variables, which are introduced by FOR, can be removed from the WHERE expression and substituted with a context item expression (.). The substitution is prohibitive whenever the new context item reference conflicts with an update of the context item at runtime, which is e.g. the case if the checked variable is enclosed in a deeper predicate, or specified in the middle of a path expression. The occurrence test can be safely skipped for sub-expressions if the variable is shadowed by another variable with the same name.

If the checks are successful, WHERE is rewritten as shown in Algorithm 11:

- **Line 1**: The WHERE expression is stored in *tests*. If it is a logical AND expression, it is replaced by its arguments, as single predicates can be optimized more easily in subsequent steps[7].

- **Line 2**: An array *targets* is created, which, for all tests, contains pointers to the variable bindings (i.e., the expression of the FOR or LET clause). By default, all pointers are set to 0 and thus reference the first (outermost) binding.

- **Line 3-13**: The most suitable FOR binding is now chosen for all tests, and will be stored in *best*: A second loop starts from the innermost binding. If the binding is a FOR clause, it is selected as new *best* candidate. If the current test uses the variable in question at least once, the binding referenced as *best* is chosen as target for attaching the test, and the check of the remaining, outer bindings is skipped. If no best target candidate has been selected yet, which happens, e.g., if the innermost

---

[7] A single predicate, in which multiple tests are combined with an AND expression, can as well be represented via multiple predicates, provided that no positional predicates are used.

3.3. Optimizations

Algorithm 11 FLWOR.CompileWhere()
1 $tests :=$ expressions specified in WHERE clause
2 $targets :=$ integer array, initialized with 0
3 **for** $t := 0$ **to** $\#tests - 1$ **do**
4    $best :=$ null
5   **for** $b := \#$BINDINGS $- 1$ **to** 0 **do**
6      $best := b$ **if** BINDINGS$[b]$ is a For clause
7   **if** $tests[t]$ uses BINDINGS$[b]$.VAR **then**
8   **return if** $best =$ null
9        $targets[t] := best$
10   **break**
11   **end if**
12   **end for**
13 **end for**
14 **for** $t := 0$ **to** $\#tests - 1$ **do**
15   $bind :=$ BINDINGS$[targets[t]]$
16   $expr := tests[t]$ with all $bind$.VAR references replaced by a context item
17   wrap $expr$ with `fn:boolean()` function if type is numeric
18   add $expr$ as predicate to $bind$.EXPR
19 **end for**
20 eliminate WHERE clause

- variable is declared by a LET clause, the optimization is canceled. If none of the variables is used by the test, it will be evaluated by the outermost binding.

- **Line 14-17**: In a second loop over all tests, the target binding for the current test is stored in $bind$. All references of the target variable in the test are recursively substituted by a context item. If static typing indicates that the expression $expr$ will yield a numeric result, it is wrapped with a `fn:boolean()` function to prevent that the evaluated value will be mistaken as a positional test.

- **Line 18**: If the existing expression $bind$.EXPR is a path expression, $expr$ will be attached as a predicate to the last axis step. If the expression is a filter expression, $expr$ will be added as a predicate to this expression. Otherwise, the expression will be converted to a filter expression with $expr$ attached as single predicate.

- **Line 20**: Finally, WHERE is removed from the FLWOR expression.

As indicated before, the substitution process will never attach predicates to inner LET clauses. The following query demonstrates the need to differ between FOR and LET:

Original: `for $a in 1 let $b := 2 where $b = 3 return $a`
Modified: `for $a in 1 let $b := 2[. = 3] return $a`

3.3. Optimizations

The first query returns an empty sequence, as the comparison in the WHERE clause will never be true. The second query, in which the WHERE expression has been attached to the LET clause, returns 1, as LET will always cause one iteration, no matter if zero or more items are bound to b. If a WHERE expression is attached to an outermost LET clause, however, the query remains correct as the attached predicate will be independent from all inner bindings.

After the WHERE clause has been replaced, the inlining of variables, as described in 3.3.1.2, might lead to a complete elimination of the FLWOR expression: The query presented in the beginning of this section will be automatically rewritten to its XPath equivalent; see Figure 3.5 for the original and the optimized query plans.

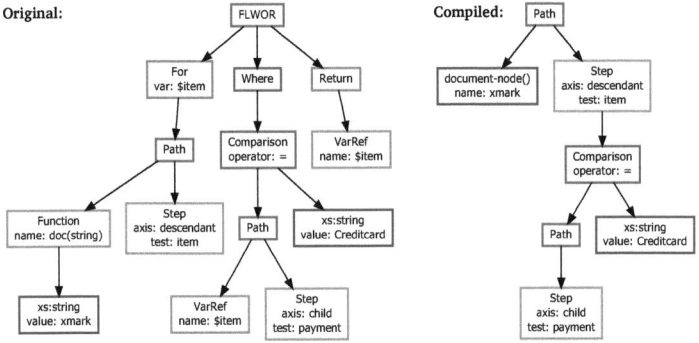

Figure 3.5: FLWOR expression: original and optimized query

3.3.2 Index Optimizations

Many location paths contain predicates with comparison operators to match XML elements or attributes with specific contents. The expression //country[@name="Japan"] is an example for a query with a comparison operator, which returns all country elements of a document with a name attribute and a value Japan. As indicated in Section 2.6.3, value indexes can be used to speed up queries of this kind, if meta data and the statistics of a database indicate that an index access is possible and expected to be cheaper than scan-based query evaluation.

3.3. Optimizations

Strictly speaking, in the context of this work, the index-supported rewriting of expressions is a static query optimization. An extra subsection has been added, though, to do justice to its complexity. The challenges are threefold:

1. A path expression needs to be uniquely *correlated* with a database, or documents in a database, at compile time.

2. Predicates of all steps of a path expression need to be *analyzed* if they are candidates for index access.

3. The path expression needs to be *rewritten*, such that the index access will be performed first, followed by the evaluation of the inverted location path.

With regard to relational databases, Step 2 bears some resemblance with the rewriting of selections, whereas Step 1 and 3 would be void operations, as relational data is limited to flat tables, with indexes being uniquely coupled with columns of these tables. Next, XQuery is more versatile than SQL – which is both an advantage and a drawback. As an example, the following query cannot be rewritten to access the index of a single database, as it defines various documents and paths as input:

```
for $in in (doc('input')/path/to/relevant/nodes,
            doc('http://remote.input')//section,
            <xml>dynamically created input</xml>)
where $in/text() = 'one'
return <hit>{ $in }</hit>
```

3.3.2.1 Database Context

Algorithm 12 shows a (simplified) solution for Challenge 1. It returns the initial context value for an expression, which might in turn contain the reference to the database that will be accessed at runtime:

The *query context*, containing both static and dynamic information on the query, is passed on as an argument. It includes a reference to the current *context value*[8]. The algorithm will return a value that depends on the kind of the first step of the path expression:

---

[8]The XQuery Specification [BCF+07] defines a *context item*, which is the currently processed item during query evaluation. In the scope of this work, the concept was generalized, and the item was replaced by a *context value*, which may contain several items such as, e.g., a sequence of document nodes. Note that this modification has no effects on the conformance with the other language features.

3.3. Optimizations

Algorithm 12 Path.GetContext(*context*: QueryContext) : Value
---
Require: STEPS = array with all path steps
1   *first*:=STEPS[0]
2   **if** *first* is a Root **then**
3   **return** *first*.evaluate(*context*.VALUE)
4   **else if** *first* is a Value **then**
5   **return** *first* as Value
6   **else if** *first* is an AxisStep **then**
7   **return** *context*.VALUE
8   **end if**
9   **return** null

- **Line 2-3**: if the step is a root expression, the document node of the current context value is evaluated and returned.
  Example: /node consists of a root expression and a child step.

- **Line 4-5**: if the first step is a value, it will be returned as a result. This value might be a document node resulting from a pre-evaluated doc() function.
  Example: doc('input')/node consists of a document function and a child step.

- **Line 6-7**: if the first step is an ordinary axis step, the current context value is returned, as it will be used for evaluating this step.
  Example: node consists of a single child step.

- **Line 9**: null is returned, if none of the cases applies.

The context value will be temporarily set to this new value, and will be reset to its original value after the remaining optimization steps have been performed. If all items of the value are nodes that refer to the same database, this database reference will serve as input for the subsequent steps; if not, the process is canceled.

3.3.2.2 Predicate Analysis

Expressions that are suitable for index rewritings may occur in all predicates of all steps of a path. Numerous kinds of expressions are of interest, such as:

- Equality expressions: /library/medium[type = ('Journal', 'Paper')]
- Range expressions: //year[text() > 2000]/../title
- Full-text requests: //medium/title[text() contains text "L'Étranger"]
- Logical expressions (AND, OR): //medium[(type = 'DVD' or type = 'Video') and title contains text 'chien andalou']

3.3. Optimizations

If all predicates have been parsed, multiple rewriting candidates might be found. While it is possible to convert all of those predicates to access indexes, various real-life workloads have shown that, on average, much better results can be expected if only one predicate is rewritten[9]. This is what happens in Algorithm 13: All steps and predicates of a path expression are parsed. An index context c is created, containing meta information for rewriting a predicate for index access. If a predicate can be rewritten, c is chosen as a new return candidate if no other candidate has been found yet or if it is cheaper than the previous candidate. Finally, the *context* variable is returned, which contains the optimal index candidate, or a `null` reference.

Algorithm 13 Path.IndexContext(*data*: Data) : IndexContext

Require: STEPS = array with all path steps
1 $context := $ `null`
2 **for** *step* **in** STEPS **do**
3   **continue if** *step* is no AxisStep
4   **for** *pred* **in** *step*.PREDICATES **do**
5      $c := $ new IndexContext(*data, pred, step*)
6   **continue if not** *pred*.IndexAccessible(c)
7   **if** $context = $ `null` **or** $c.costs < context.costs$ **then**
8        $context := c$
9   **return** *context* **if** $context.costs = 0$
10   **end if**
11   **end for**
12 **end for**
13 **return** *context*

In the scope of our work, *costs* are defined as positive integer values, representing the exact or estimated number of returned index results. If costs are zero ($costs = 0$), the index will return no results at all, and the whole path expression can be replaced with an empty sequence at compile time. If the estimated costs exceed a certain maximum value, such as the number of text nodes in the database, index access can be skipped in favor of a standard query execution.

By default, the IndexAccessible(c) method returns `false`. It is overwritten by all expressions that enable the query to be rewritten. Due to the complexity of XQuery, many additional checks have to be performed to decide if index access is possible, and what costs it will cause. For equality tests, which are defined by the general comparison ex-

---
[9]Note that a single predicate may still result in several index calls, e.g., if several equality comparisons are specified within a logical expression.

3.3. Optimizations

pression, the following preconditions must be given (examples for invalid expressions have been added):

1. The operator tests for *equality*(=). *Invalid*: [text() != 'A']
2. One of the operands is a path with *axis steps* only, concluded with a text() or attribute step. *Invalid*: [replace(@id, 'A', '') = '123'] or [step = 'A']
3. Depending on the *kind* test of the last step, the database has an up-to-date *index structure* for texts or attribute values.
4. The second operand contains no reference to the current *context* item or position. *Invalid*: [text() = .]
5. All resulting items of the second operand are *strings*, or untyped atomics (including nodes) that can be cast to strings. *Invalid*: [text() = ('A', 123)]

If all tests are successful, and if the strings to be matched are atomic values, the index can be accessed in advance to evaluate the exact number of results, which will be set as costs for the index operation. If multiple strings are specified, the number of results will be summarized. Otherwise, if the search strings are unknown at compile time (e.g. if the search expression is a variable), a constant percentage of the number of database nodes will be set to indicate that an index access is assumed to be cheaper than sequential database scanning. – More details on individual expressions, which can be rewritten for index access, are included in the summary in Section 3.5.

3.3.2.3 Path Inversion

In the scope of this work, a bottom-up approach is pursued, in which the index is accessed first, followed by the evaluation of all other predicate tests and axis steps. All location steps in the selected predicate and the main path have to be *inverted* to ensure that the expression yields the correct results. This inversion is possible for many paths, as numerous symmetries exist between location paths. For example, the following location paths are equivalent [OMFB02]:

1. descendant-or-self::m[child::n] ≡ descendant::n/parent::m
2. p[self::n]/parent::m ≡ p/self::n/parent::m
3. self::m[child::n] ≡ child::n/parent::m

As the three cited equivalences imply, it is not sufficient to just replace all steps with their inverse counterparts. Instead, some steps will be enclosed by a new predicate, and others will be moved out of an existing predicate. Some queries with a *descendant* step and a predicate, which can be rewritten for index access, are the following:

3.3. Optimizations

4. /descendant::m[child::text() = e] ≡ TI(e)/parent::m
5. /descendant::m[descendant::text() = e] ≡ TI(e)/ancestor::m
6. /descendant::m[child::n/child::text() = e] ≡ TI(e)/parent::n/parent::m
7. /descendant::m[descendant::n/child::text() = e] ≡ TI(e)/parent::n/ancestor::m
8. /descendant::m[child::n/descendant::text() = e] ≡ TI(e)/ancestor::n/parent::m

Note that all expressions start from the root node. TI(e) is a shortcut for a index function that returns all text nodes from the index, matching the string value of e. The expression is rewritten from right to left: the axis of each step is inverted and combined with the node test of its left-hand step. The first step is ignored, as all descendant nodes have a root node. The rewritings have similar characteristics for attribute tests:

9. /descendant::m[attribute::* = e] ≡ AI(e)/parent::m
10. /descendant::m[attribute::n = e] ≡ AI(e, n)/parent::m

AI(e) represents an index function for attribute values. While Query 9 selects all attributes to be included in the equality test, an additional argument is added in the index function in Query 10 to filter the results to the specified attribute. The following query contains a full-text expression:

11. /descendant::m[child::text() contains text e] ≡ FI(e)/parent::m

FI(e) is a placeholder for the index-based evaluation of all kinds of full-text queries. As indicated in 3.1.3, XQuery Full Text offers much more features than simple term lookups. As most of the full-text index operations comply with the general rewritings[10], the following equivalence rules will be restricted to text nodes. In the following queries, additional steps are attached to the main path:

12. /descendant::m/child::n[child::text() = e] ≡ TI(e)/parent::n[parent::m]
13. /descendant::m/child::n/child::o[child::text() = e] ≡
    TI(e)/parent::o[parent::n/parent::m]

The added steps trigger the creation of a new predicate: Let s be the step that defines the predicate relevant for index access. All steps before s are inverted in the same way as already shown, and the resulting path is enclosed in a new predicate. An additional root test has to be attached to the predicate if the path starts with a *child* step:

14. /child::m[child::text() = e] ≡ TI(e)/parent::m[parent::document-node()]

---

[10]The only exception to this rule is the handling of negated queries, such as e.g. //*[text() contains text ftnot 'A'], in which a hybrid approach is taken to both benefit from the index and sequential processing. More specifics on evaluating full-text predicates, and its implications for index-based processing, are found in [Gat09] and [GGHS09a].

3.3. Optimizations

15. /child::m/child::n[child::text() = e] ≡
    TI(e)/parent::n[parent::m/parent::document-node()]
16. /child::m/descendant::n[child::text() = e] ≡
    TI(e)/parent::n[ancestor::m/parent::document-node()]

The final document-node() test filters all nodes that do not start from the root node. The following example demonstrates the difference between *descendant* and *child* steps:

Document:	<a>XX</a>
Query:	/descendant::*[child::text() = 'X']
Compiled:	TI('X')/parent::*
Result:	<a>XX</a>, X
Query:	/child::*[child::text() = 'X']
Compiled:	TI('X')/parent::*[parent::document-node()]
Result:	<a>XX</a>

TI('X') returns two text nodes as result, and the subsequent location step yields the parent elements. While the [ancestor::document-node()] predicate can be omitted for the first query, as all elements have a document node as ancestor, the document test is mandatory for the second query to filter out the second result node.

17. /child::m[child::text() = e][p] ≡ TI(e)/parent::m[parent::document-node()][p]
18. /child::m[child::text() = e]/s ≡ TI(e)/parent::m[parent::document-node()]/s
19. /descendant::m[child::text() = e][p]/s ≡ TI(e)/parent::m[p]/s
20. /descendant::n[p]/child::m[child::text() = e]/s ≡
    TI(e)/parent::m[parent::n[p]]/s

The last four queries show that remaining predicates and steps need no special treatment. They are simply added to the newly created expression. The same accounts for predicates of inverted steps, which are adopted without changes.

Concluding this section, we observed that the index rewritings have turned out to be the most important optimizations to make the system capable of answering queries on very large documents in interactive time. The speedup of equi-joins is particularly helpful if the equality operands are not fully known and evaluated at runtime, which is e.g. the case if the string to be matched is wrapped into a variable. Section 3.6 will present some examples of queries that benefit from index rewritings.

3.3.3 Runtime Optimizations

All static optimizations, which have been presented throughout this section, have constant or logarithmic costs and will be cheaper than the query evaluation step, at least in most cases. Next to that, they will only be performed once at compile time. As not all properties of the touched data will be known before the query is evaluated – or cannot be used for optimizations – some decisions have to be taken at runtime, or *just-in-time*. As an example, a sequence might include items of different types, and an expression will need to choose between different evaluation plans at runtime. Next, the contents of a document may be used as input for another doc() function, as the following example demonstrates:

```
for $db in doc('list.xml')//database/@name return doc($db)
```

Dynamic query processing is a well-known topic in the database world; see [GW89] for an important contribution on dynamic evaluation plans. A major challenge is to quickly decide which evaluation alternative will possibly yield the fastest results: otherwise, the costs for finding the cheapest step might outweigh the costs for evaluating the original, unoptimized query expression.

In the scope of this work, two practical runtime optimizations have been picked out to demonstrate that simple runtime tests, backed by appropriate extensions of the evaluation framework, can have a strong impact on the execution time. Some benchmark results are listed in 4.2.1.

3.3.3.1 Direct Sequence Access

XQuery allows users to write code that looks similar to procedural code:

```
declare variable $data := doc('input.xml')//data
for $i in 1 to count($data)
return $data[$i]
```

The query example generates a sequence of data elements, and the subsequent FLWOR expressions returns all items of the sequence[11]. While the bracket notation looks like a classical array offset, it is in fact a predicate containing a positional test – which is a special case in XQuery, as a predicate may contain arbitrary expressions. Hence, if the query is evaluated in a straightforward manner, and if data has n elements, the predicate will be matched against all items of the sequence n times, resulting in $\Theta(n^2)$ (both best and worst case).

---

[11]Obviously, the variable reference $data would yield the same result as the FLWOR expression.

3.3. Optimizations

As a positional predicate will never yield more than one result, a first optimization consists in adding a skip mechanism to the predicate test, which will be triggered at runtime after the first positional test has been successful. This will reduce costs to an average of $\mathcal{O}(\frac{n^2}{2})$. In practice, however, this optimization yields much better costs as results are often limited to the first m elements of a sequence, in which case the costs are further lowered to $\mathcal{O}(\frac{m^2}{2})$.

If all items of a sequence are available at runtime, the data structure storing the sequence can be extended by methods to directly access items by their offset. While this concept does not harmonize with iterative, pipelined query evaluation (see 3.4.1), it perfectly goes hand in hand with pre-evaluated sequences, such as found in global variables, or in parts of the query which are repeatedly evaluated and thus cached, and the resulting costs will be $\mathcal{O}(n)$.

To decide if positional access is possible in a filter expression, such as the one shown in the example and described in the Summary (3.5), the predicate is evaluated at runtime. If it yields a single positive integer – which might as well be true for a double number without fractional digits, a case which cannot be covered with static typing – and if the value of the main expression has already been evaluated and is fully available for positional access, i.e., if the sequence contains a method for direct access, the relevant item is requested and returned as single result. If no direct access is available, a new iterator is created, which will be aborted as soon as the first result has been returned. If the predicate is not numeric, or if the predicate expression depends on the current context, or if more than one predicate has been defined for the filter expression, the standard evaluation path is taken, which supports both positional and boolean predicates.

3.3.3.2 General Comparisons

General comparisons are one of the most frequently used expressions in XQuery; accordingly, small optimizations can lead to significant performance boosts. In the specification, they are defined as "existentially quantified comparisons", which atomize the items of both its operands and return true if one single comparison is successful. As a result, comparisons with empty sequences, such as () = () or () != (), return false whereas (1,2) > (2,1) returns true. As a general comparison with $m * n$ items will have a worst case of $\mathcal{O}(m * n)$, one of the item sequences needs to be iterated several times, and better performance can be expected if the intermediate results are cached. Caching may be suboptimal, however, if only single items are to be compared (which are the types of comparisons that occur most often in practice). Depending on the cardinality of the operands, the best evaluation variant can be chosen step by step at runtime (note that details on iterative processing can be found in the upcoming Section 3.4.1):

1. If static typing indicates that both operands will yield 0 or 1 results, the expression can be optimized at compile time: the atomic values from both operands can be directly compared without further cardinality checks.

2. Otherwise, an iterator *iter*1 is requested for the first operand. If *iter*1 indicates that 0 results are expected, `false` is returned.

3. If *iter*1 indicates 1 result, and if static typing indicates that the second operand will return 0 or 1 results, the first item of *iter*1 will be compared with the atomic value of the second operand. Otherwise, the second iterator *iter*2 is requested, and `false` is returned if the iterator will return 0 results.

4. If both iterators indicate 1 result, the firsts items that are returned by the iterators are compared.

5. If the number of results for *iter*1 is unknown, and if *iter*2 will return 1 result, all items from *iter*1 are compared with the first item from *iter*2.

6. If none of the cases applies, all results from *iter*1 are compared with the first item from *iter*2 and cached for repeated access. If no comparison was successful, the cached items are compared with all other items from *iter*2.

While each of the listed conditions, except for the first, adds some computation overhead at runtime, it does not outbalance the time needed for caching or reiterating all items of an iterator.

3.4 Evaluation

After all normalizations and optimizations have been performed, the resulting expression tree contains all information needed to evaluate the query. In the evaluation step, all data will be handled that cannot be statically processed. As was shown in the previous section on query optimization, this step can be reduced to simply returning the result of a compiled query – which is often the case if the query is supposed to return statistical information on a database, using the `fn:count()` function, or if a query does not use database references at all.

3.4. Evaluation

Note that classical teaching on compiler construction allows for an additional code generation step, which transforms an expression tree into executable code. This step is mandatory if the compiled code is materialized and executed later. In the context of XQuery, it has been applied to Qexo [Bot04], BEA/XQRL [FHK+03] and the Pathfinder [GMR+07]. Next, the commercial version of SAXON includes an option to generate Java byte code, which promises an average speedup of 25% [Kay08]. In the scope of this work, code generation is skipped. Instead, the generated expression tree is always evaluated directly after it has been compiled and optimized.

3.4.1 Iterative Processing

Iterative query processing is a well-known evaluation strategy in query languages [FG89, Gra93]. In the literature on XQuery, no clear distinction is made between *iterative*, *streaming*, and *pipelined* processing. In this work, the term *iterative* has been selected as favorite term, as it constitutes a link to original database publications, which share many commonalities with today's algorithms. Ideally, iterative processing results in constant CPU and I/O costs, as no intermediate results are generated that end up in much smaller final results. As an example, the query (1 to 100*1000*1000)[1] consists of a filter expression with one predicate. It returns the first of 100 million items. If the query is executed in a trivial way, the range expression will generate a sequence of 100 million integers. In the second step, all integers will be filtered by the predicate, and only the first one will be accepted as result. While the presented query may seem hypothetical, it is supposed to demonstrate that queries on large documents can cause out-of-memory errors, even if the final results are very small. *Lazy evaluation* is a related concept, which is made possible by iterative evaluation [Joh84]: computation of values can be delayed, or completely avoided, if they will not contribute to the final result. In the upper example, only the first item needs to be generated and tested, as the remaining values can be skipped (see also Section 3.3.3.1 on optimizations for speeding up positional predicates).

In its core, an iterator can be reduced to a single *Next()* method, which returns the next item of a computed expression, or a `null` reference if the iterator is exhausted and no more items are available. The iterator method can either be directly added to each expression or wrapped into an iterator object. In the iterator model of the presented query architecture, the latter variant was chosen: Each expression is extended by an *Iterator()* method, which creates and returns a new iterator instance with a *Next()* method. While the instantiation of new iterator objects consumes additional CPU time

3.4. Evaluation

and memory resources, it enables the use of singleton expressions and values, which are used in different contexts throughout the expression tree. As an example, the compiled version of the arithmetic expression 1 + 1 can be easily optimized to reference the same integer object in memory. If the iterator was part of the expression, the first call to *Next()* call would return the integer in question, and another call for the second operand would return null. The adaptive approach presented in 3.4.1.2 will show how the costs for creating new objects can be amortized in practice.

The iterator interface is extended by additional, optional methods:

- *Size()* returns the number of iterated items, or -1 if the size is unknown.
- *Get(int)* retrieves the specified item if the number of items is known, or null if no positional access is possible.
- *Reset()* resets the iterator to the first item and returns true, or false if reset is not supported.
- *Reverse()* reverses the order of the iterated items and returns true, or false if reversion is not supported.
- *Finish()* returns a sequence with all (remaining) iterated items.

While a default iterator is restricted to return only the next item of an expression, some iterators can pass on existing information on the expected output. For instance, the range expression returns a sequence of consecutive integers. As the minimum and maximum values are known when the iterator is created, the implementation of *Size()*, *Get()*, and *Reset()* is trivial. *Size()* will e.g. be called by the XQuery fn:count() function, the evaluation of which is shown in Algorithm 14: If the iterator, which is returned by the function's argument, is a value different to -1, it represents the final results. Otherwise, all items need to be iterated and counted. This way, expressions such as count(1 to 100) can be evaluated in constant time.

Size() and *Get(int)* are called by a number of other expressions:

- If the iterator size is known, and if a positional predicate is specified in the predicate of a path or filter expression, the requested item can be directly accessed and returned. If the fn:last() function is used, the last returned item can be accessed by calling $iter.Get(iter.Size()-1)$. As a consequence, the query (1 to 100)[last()] can be evaluated without actually touching the iterator items.
- The fn:subsequence($e,$s,$l) function takes expression $e and returns a new subsequence of length $l, starting at position $s. Again, the relevant items are

3.4. Evaluation

Algorithm 14 Count.Item() : Item

Require: EXPR := argument of the count function
1   $iter$:= EXPR.Iterator()
2   c := $iter$.Size()
3   **if** $c = -1$ **then**
4   **repeat**
5         $c := c + 1$
6   **until** $iter$.Next() = null
7   **end if**
8   **return** new Integer(c)

---

directly accessed with *Get(int)*. *Next()*, *Size()* and *Get()* are also implemented in the iterator, which is returned by the `fn:subsequence()` function. As a result, nested expressions such as `fn:count(fn:subsequence(1 to 100, 10, 20))` can as well be evaluated in constant time.

- The `fn:reverse($e)` function reverses the order of all items from expression $e. If all items can be accessed with *Get(int)*, there is no need to cache the incoming sequence.

Reset() is needed to iterate through the same sequence several times. This method is e.g. called by the general comparison, which compares two sequences item by item (see 3.3.3.2). If the available iterator cannot be reset, the items are first cached in a general-purpose iterator (see 3.4.1.1), which supports all mandatory and optional iterator methods.

The *Reverse()* method is called by the `fn:reverse($e)` function. If the items of a sequence can be reversed, no additional operation is necessary, as the same iterator can be returned. The range expression can be easily reversed by swapping the minimum and maximum value. As a result, the query `reverse(1 to 100)` causes no extra costs.

3.4.1.1 Caching

The caching of items cannot always be avoided. It is needed for *blocking* operators, which repeatedly access the same items returned by an iterator. Examples are the ORDER or GROUP clause in the FLWOR expression, the general comparison, some filter expression with multiple predicates, or variables, which are referenced multiple times in a query.

While most expressions contain their own iterator implementations, some iterators have been added that cache the iterated items and support all sequence operations. The *ItemIterator* is a general-purpose implementation of the iterator interface. An *Add(item)* method allows to cache single items. *Add(iterator)* consumes and caches all items of the specified iterator. If the specified iterator is already an *ItemIterator* instance, its cached items will be directly adopted. The cached items can be converted to a result sequence without being copied.

Algorithm 15 NodeIterator.Add(Node n)

Require:
    NODES := array with cached nodes
    ORDERED indicates if cached nodes are ordered and duplicate-free (*normalized*)
    RANDOM indicates if incoming nodes may invalidate order
1   $iter$:= EXPR.Iterator()
2   c := $iter$.Size()
3   **if** RANDOM and ORDERED and #NODES > 0 **then**
4   diff := n.ID − NODES[#NODES - 1].ID
5   **if** diff = 0 **then**
6   **return**
7   **else if** diff < 0 **then**
8   ORDERED = false
9   **end if**
10 **end if**
11 add n to NODES

According to the specification, the resulting nodes of location steps and combining node operators (union, intersect, except) have to fulfill two properties: they must be in document order and free of duplicates [BCF⁺07]. These requirements may cause additional costs and should thus be skipped if nodes are known to be sorted and duplicate-free (for the sake of simplicity, we will call a set of nodes *ordered* if both properties are true). If this guarantee can be given at compile time, the nodes will not be cached at all; instead, expressions will be iteratively evaluated (see 3.4.1.3 for details). Otherwise, the *NodeIterator* is applied, which ensures that all returned nodes will be ordered. If a new instance of this iterator is created, an ORDERED flag is set to true, indicating that, by default, all cached nodes are ordered. A RANDOM flag is set by the calling expression to indicate that the incoming nodes might destroy document order. If a new node is added via *Add(Node)* (see Algorithm 15), and if both the ORDERED and RANDOM flag is true, the

3.4. Evaluation

id value of the node is compared with the *id* of its predecessor[12]. If the *ids* are equal, the new node can be ignored, as it has already been cached. Otherwise, if the new *id* is smaller, the ORDERED flag is invalidated, and the cached nodes will be sorted and freed from duplicates as soon as the first node is requested via the iterator methods. If the nodes will not be accessed, sorting and duplicate removal can be completely avoided.

3.4.1.2 Adaptive Approach

For non-blocking operators, it appears reasonable at first glance to apply iterative query processing whenever possible. There are some cases, however, in which the iterative concept turns out to be suboptimal. First of all, care must be taken with expressions that perform disk-based operations: if a single iterator call can trigger a selective disk-access, and if it is followed by a second selective access somewhere else on disk, this can lead to pseudo-random access patterns, which are much slower than sequential calls. The index equivalents of the following queries demonstrate the difference:

1. `//text()[. = ("a", "z")]` ≡ `TextIndex("a") | TextIndex("z")`
2. `//*[text() = "a"]` ≡ `TextIndex("a")/parent::*`

The first query performs two index operations, the results of which are joined by a union expression, and the second expression accesses an index and passes on the results to a parent step. Preliminary performance tests on these queries were indicating that the iterative retrieval of single index results (which essentially are *pre* values, possibly followed by *pos* values for full-text requests) performed much worse than a conventional retrieval, in which the cached *pre* values are wrapped by an iterator.

Next, many expressions, such as arithmetic operators or value comparisons, expect single items as input. If the resulting item of an operand is first wrapped into an iterator, which is later requested by a single item call, the iterator concept represents an obvious overhead needed to fulfill the demands of the overall architecture.

An adaptive approach has been chosen in our architecture to overcome the potential bottlenecks: The abstract Expression class, which is the super class of all expressions, is extended by an additional *Item()* method, which returns the evaluated value as a single item, or a `null` reference for an empty sequence. If the expression evaluates to

---

[12]For fragments, *ids* are generated at runtime; for disk-based nodes, the database reference and the *pre* value is used to compute equality.

3.4. Evaluation

more than one item, a type error is raised. This method is called by all expressions that accept at most one item as result, and it is implemented by all expressions that are guaranteed to return at most one result. As a complement, the *Iterator()* method is only implemented if more than one item may be returned, and it is only called by expressions that expect sequences as result. At least one of the two methods needs to be implemented by each expression.

There will be many cases in which an expression requests a single item, but the called expression offers only an iterator implementation, or, the other way round, in which expressions request a sequence whereas the operand is only prepared to return single items. To guarantee that all expressions will be correctly served, the Expression class offers standard implementations for both methods, which come into play if they are not overwritten by the implementing expression:

Algorithm 16 Expression.Iterator() : Iterator

```
1   item := Item()
2   if item is null then
3       return empty iterator
4   else
5       return item.Iterator()
6   end if
```

In Algorithm 16, the *Item()* method of the expression is called and an iterator is wrapped around the evaluated item. If the expression is a null reference, an empty iterator is returned.

Algorithm 17 Expression.Item() : Item

```
1   iter := Iterator()
2   item := iter.Next()
3   if item is null then
4       return null
5   else if iter.Next() is null then
6       return item
7   else
8       raise type error (XPTY0004)
9   end if
```

Algorithm 17 calls the *Iterator()* method of the expression and requests the first item. null is returned if the iterator is exhausted after the first call. If the iterator returns no second item, the first item is returned as result. Otherwise, a type error is raised, which indicates that at most one item is allowed at this stage.

3.4. Evaluation

Algorithm 18 Expression.Ebv() : boolean

```
1   if expression returns zero items then
2       return false
3   else if expression returns one item then
4       return Item().Boolean()
5   else
6       iter := Iterator()
7       item := iter.Next()
8       if item is null then
9           return false
10      else if item is no node and iter.Next() is not null then
11          raise type error (FORG0006)
12      else
13          return item.Boolean()
14      end if
15  end if
```

Two supplementary methods have been added to speed up the non-iterative evaluation. Algorithm 18 computes the *effective boolean value* of an expression: If static typing indicates that zero items will be returned, evaluation is skipped and `false` is returned. If one item can be expected, the boolean value of the result of *Item()* is computed. Otherwise, if the exact number of results is unknown or more than one, *Iterator()* is called, and the first item is requested. `false` is returned if this item is a `null` reference. In accordance with the specification, an error is raised if the first item is no node, and if the iterator returns additional items. Otherwise, the boolean value of the first item is returned.

Algorithm 19 Expression.Value() : Value

```
1   if expression returns zero items then
2       return  empty sequence
3   else if expression returns one item then
4       return Item()
5   else
6       return Iterator().Finish()
7   end if
```

Algorithm 19 is called whenever the complete value of an expression is needed. This is e.g. the case for global variables, which are only evaluated once. Again, the iterator will only be called if the expression might return more than one item.

3.4.1.3 Expressions

As XQuery embraces more than 50 expressions and operators, and more than 100 functions, a complete listing of all iterative implementations and optimizations would be soporific. Instead, we picked out distinctive expressions to demonstrate the general benefits of iterative processing. In 3.4.2, additional details are given on the iterative traversal of location paths.

Algorithm 20 Intersect.Iterator.Next() : Node

Require: ITERATORS := array with iterators on all operands
1 $nodes$:= array with cached nodes
2 **for** $i := 0$ **to** #ITERATORS-1 **do**
3      $nodes[i]$:= ITERATORS$[i]$.Next()
4   **return** null **if** $nodes[i]$ is null
5 **end for**
6 $i := 1$
7 **while** $i <$ #$nodes$ **do**
8      $diff := nodes[0]$.ID $- nodes[i]$.ID
9   **if** $diff < 0$ **then**
10         $nodes[0]$:=ITERATORS[0].Next()
11   **return** null **if** $nodes[0]$ is null
12         $i := 1$
13   **else if** $diff > 0$ **then**
14         $nodes[i]$:=ITERATORS$[i]$.Next()
15   **return** null **if** $nodes[i]$ is null
16   **else**
17         $i := i + 1$
18   **end if**
19 **end while**
20 **return** $nodes[0]$

The classical database operators, which can be processed in a streamlined fashion if the incoming items are *ordered* (see 3.4.1.1), are Union, Intersect and Except. The Intersect expression is described in more detail: Algorithm 20 depicts the *Next()* function of the returned iterator. First, all nodes are cached, which are returned by calls to the *Next()* method of the iterators of the operands. As soon as one operand returns a null reference in this and all subsequent steps, evaluation is stopped, as intersect will return no more results. In the following *while* loop, the node identity (ID) of all cached nodes is compared one by one. If a node has a smaller ID than the others, its successor is requested. If all nodes have the same ID, one node is returned, and the others are

3.4. Evaluation

discarded.

Algorithm 21 Filter.Iterator.Next() : Item

Require:
    PREDS := filter predicates
    CONTEXT := query context
    ITERATOR := iterator, generated on the input sequence
    POS := 0 (current context position)
1   cache context value and position
2   **loop**
3   POS := POS + 1
4   *item* := ITERATOR.Next()
5   **break if** *item* = null
6   CONTEXT.VALUE := *item*
7   CONTEXT.POS := POS
8   **for** *pred* **in** PREDS **do**
9   **break if** the *truth value* of *pred* is false
10   **end for**
11   **break if** all predicates tests were successful
12   **end loop**
13   restore context value and position
14   **return** *item*

The filter expression was chosen as second example; its iterative variant is presented in Algorithm 21. A filter is introduced by a primary expression and followed by one or more predicates. If more than one position test is specified in the predicate list, the context position may be different for each predicate. As an example, the query (1 to 3) [2] [1] will yield 2, as the context position in the second predicate refers to the results of the first predicate. This is why the depicted iterator only yields valid results if the positional test is defined as first predicate, or if no position predicate is specified at all. If the *Next()* method is called, the current context value and position are cached. In the infinite loop, the next item from the primary iterator is set as new context item, along with the updated context position. All predicates are then applied on the current context. If a predicate test fails, the remaining tests are skipped. If all tests have been successful, however, the loop is interrupted, the old context is restored and the result is returned. The same happens if the iterator does not return any more results.

XQuery functions may benefit from iterative processing as well. The following functions – and many others – consume and return sequences:

- index-of($seq, $item) returns the positions of a specific item in a sequence.

3.4. Evaluation

- `insert-before($seq, $pos, $ins)` inserts a new sequence in a sequence.
- `remove($seq, $pos)` removes an item at a specific position.
- `reverse($seq)` reverses the order of the items in a sequence.
- `subsequence($seq, $start, $len)` returns a sub-sequence.
- `distinct-values($seq)` returns all distinct values of a sequence.

Algorithm 22 IndexOf.Iterator.Next() : Item

Require:
    ITERATOR := iterator on the input sequence (`$seq`)
    ITEM := item to be found (`$item`)
    POS := 0 (current iterator position)
1 **loop**
2   POS := POS + 1
3    $item$:= ITERATOR.Next()
4   **if** $item$ = null **then**
5   **return** null
6   **else if** ITEM equals $item$ **then**
7   **return** new Integer(POS)
8   **end if**
9 **end loop**

In Algorithm 22, the *Next()* method of the iterator of the `index-of($seq, $item)` function is shown. Before the method is called, the iterator of the input sequence is assigned to ITERATOR, and the item to be found is assigned to ITEM. If *Next()* is called, a new item is requested from the sequence iterator. The infinite loop is only stopped if this item is null, or if it matches the item to be found. In the latter case, the sequence position is returned as integer. – If this method was implemented in a conventional manner, all items of the input sequence would have to be cached first, and the resulting sequence would consume additional memory.

3.4.2 Location Paths

This section discusses the evaluation of *location paths*, which are a core feature of the XPath language and the most important expression for performing queries on XML instances (see also Section 3.1.1). In XQuery, location paths are a special type of path expressions, containing only axis steps. Our algorithms for evaluating location steps on the presented table storage have initially been inspired by the Staircase Join [GvKT03], a join operator that speeds up the execution of location paths in relational databases.

3.4. Evaluation

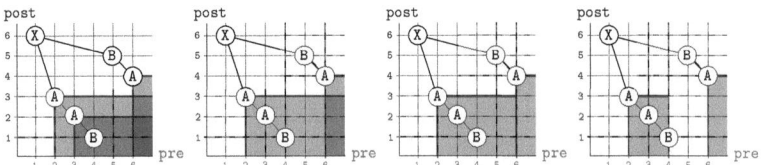

Figure 3.6: $pre/post$ planes; *descendant* step for the three A elements: a) conventional, b) with Pruning, c) with Partitioning, d) with Skipping

3.4.2.1 Staircase Join

The Staircase Join comprises three "tree aware" optimization strategies, namely *Pruning*, *Partitioning*, and *Skipping*, which complement each other and which speed up the evaluation of XPath axes for a given context node sequence. Figure 3.6 shows four $pre/post$ planes (see 2.3.2 for a reminder). The gray rectangles depict the regions that have to be scanned from left to right to evaluate a *descendant* step, starting from the three A elements with pre values 2, 3, and 6. In the first plane, some areas are scanned multiple times, resulting in quadratic costs and duplicate results. In the second region, *pruning* is applied: the axis evaluation is only performed for the first and third node: as the second node is a descendant of the first node (which can be derived from its pre and $post$ values), it is ignored, as all its descendants will already be traversed by the first node. In the *partitioned* plane, the scanned areas are made disjunct, i.e., scanning is canceled whenever the pre value of the currently scanned node equals the pre value of the next context node. In the rightmost *skipping* plane, scanning is stopped as soon as the $post$ values indicate that all descendants of the context node have been visited. For more details on the Staircase Join algorithms, the reader is referred to Grust's original publications [Gru02, GvKT03, GT04].

The Staircase Join techniques can also be adapted to other encodings: Algorithm 23 demonstrates the traversal of the *descendant* axis, based on the $pre/dist/size$ encoding. Skipping is not necessary at all, as the $size$ property of a node directly reflects the number of descendants (see 2.3.4). Next, nodes can be pruned *on-the-fly*: n_1 and n_2 designate a successive pair of context nodes. The main loop reflects the *partitioning* step. The inner loop visits all descendant nodes of n_1 and adds them to the result array. If pre equals the pre value of the next context node n_2, n_2 is discarded and overwritten by its successor. If all descendants of n_1 have been traversed, the loop is continued with n_2 until all context nodes have been processed.

3.4. Evaluation

Algorithm 23 Axis.Descendant(*nodes* : NodeSequence) : NodeSequence
1 *result* := new NodeIterator()
2 n_1 := *nodes*.Next()
3 **while** n_1 is not null **do**
4   n_2 := *nodes*.Next()
5   **for** $pre := n_1.pre$ **to** $n_1.pre + n_1.size - 1$ **do**
6   add new Node(*pre*) to *result*
7   **if** $n_2.pre = pre$ **then**
8   n_2 := *nodes*.Next()
9   **end if**
10   **end for**
11     $n_1 := n_2$
12 **end while**
13 **return** *result*

Algorithm 24 Axis.Child(*nodes* : NodeSequence) : NodeSequence
1 *result* := new NodeIterator()
2 **for** *n* in *nodes* **do**
3   **for** $pre := n.pre + n.asize$ **to** $n.pre + n.size$ **step** Size(*pre*) **do**
4   add new Node(*pre*) to *result*
5   **end for**
6 **end for**
7 **return** *result*.Sort()

The traversal of the *parent* and *ancestor* axes is very simple, as the *dist* property offers a direct reference to the relevant nodes. The evaluation of the *child* axis never generates duplicates, as each node has a unique parent. Therefore, pruned *child* nodes would yield wrong results, as all nodes of the input context need to be considered for traversal. In Algorithm 24, the children of all input nodes are evaluated. The *pre* counter in the inner loop is initialized with the sum of the *pre* value of the context node and its *asize* value, which represents the number of attributes. By incrementing *pre* by the *size* value of the currently visited node, using *Size(pre)*, all descendants of the child nodes are skipped, and only the relevant nodes are touched. The document order of the nodes might get lost in the resulting sequence, however, as the following query shows:

    <X><X>a</X>b</X>/descendant::X/child::text()

The first location step generates two context nodes X, which both have a single text node as child. As the text child of the first X element is placed after the text of the subordinate X element, the resulting text nodes (b, a) need to be sorted before they are returned. To avoid sorting, a stack can be added to the algorithm, which caches all nodes that

3.4. Evaluation

are ancestors of the currently traversed parent node (see [Rod03] for the corresponding algorithm on the *pre/post* encoding).

In practice, we observed that the Staircase Join optimizations (and particularly the *pruning* step) are relevant in only a few cases, as most queries will not generate any duplicates, or will return small result sets instead, which can be sorted and freed from duplicates without considerable overhead. Next, many location paths can be optimized in advance to avoid the generation of duplicate nodes at runtime. The most common example represent queries with two location steps `descendant::node()/child::*`, which would clearly benefit from *pruning*, but can also be rewritten to a single location step `descendant::*` (details on rewriting location paths have been discussed in 3.4). As pruning cannot be applied to location steps with position predicates [GVK04], and as XQuery allows arbitrarily complex expressions as predicates, the presented algorithms have eventually been replaced with simplified, iterative versions of the algorithms, which process context nodes one by one. If the incoming nodes are known to be sorted, and if the axis steps preserve orderedness and generate no duplicates, the complete location path can be evaluated in an iterative manner (details on the detection of duplicates and orderedness in location path can be looked up in [HMV05]). Otherwise, the steps are evaluated one after another, and the results are added to a *NodeIterator* instance, which only sorts the nodes if necessary (see Section 3.4.1.1).

3.4.2.2 Path Traversal

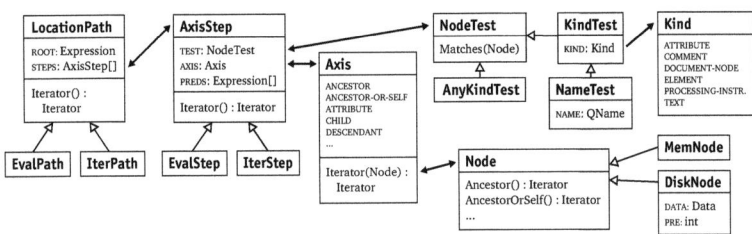

Figure 3.7: Class diagram: location path expressions

Figure 3.7 depicts the most important expressions of location paths. In this work, a *LocationPath* is specified as an expression with an optional root *Expression* and several *AxisSteps*, and an *AxisStep* consists of an *Axis*, a *NodeTest* and zero or more *Expressions* as predicates. Both the conventional and iterative versions of the *LocationPath* and *AxisStep*

3.4. Evaluation

Algorithm 25 DiskNode iterators

Require: DATA := database reference, PRE := *pre* value, P := PRE (*pre* cursor)

Child.Next() : Node
Require: P := P + DATA.ASize(P)
1 **if** P = PRE + DATA.Size(PRE)
2 **return** null
3 **end if**
4 $node$:= new DiskNode(DATA, P)
5 P := P + DATA.Size(P)
6 **return** $node$

Parent.Next() : Node
1 **if** P != PRE
2 **return** null
3 **end if**
4 P := P − DATA.Dist(P)
5 **return** new DiskNode(DATA, P)

Descendant.Next() : Node
1 P := P + DATA.ASize(P)
2 **if** P = PRE + DATA.Size(PRE)
3 **return** null
4 **end if**
5 **return** new DiskNode(DATA, P)

AncestorOrSelf.Next() : Node
1 **if** P = −1
2 **return** null
3 **end if**
4 $node$:= new DiskNode(DATA, P)
5 P := P − DATA.Dist(P)
6 **return** $node$

Following.Next() : Node
Require: P := P + DATA.Size(P)
1 **if** P = DATA.META.SIZE
2 **return** null
3 **end if**
4 $node$:= new DiskNode(DATA, P)
5 P := P + DATA.ASize(P)
6 **return** $node$

Attribute.Next() : Node
1 P := P + 1
2 **if** P = PRE + DATA.ASize(PRE)
3 **return** null
4 **end if**
5 **return** new DiskNode(DATA, P)

Self.Next() : Node
Require: EVAL := false
1 **if** EVAL
2 **return** null
3 **end if**
4 EVAL := true
5 **return** new DiskNode(DATA, P)

DescendantOrSelf.Next() : Node
1 **if** P = PRE + DATA.Size(PRE)
2 **return** null
3 **end if**
4 $node$:= new DiskNode(DATA, P)
5 P := P + DATA.ASize(P)
6 **return** $node$

Ancestor.Next() : Node
1 P := P − DATA.Dist(P)
2 **if** P = −1
3 **return** null
4 **end if**
5 **return** new DiskNode(DATA, P)

FollowingSibling.Next() : Node
Require: P := P + DATA.Size(P)
  PAR := PRE − DATA.Dist(PRE)
1 **if** P = PAR + DATA.Size(PAR)
2 **return** null
3 **end if**
4 $node$:= new DiskNode(DATA, P)
5 P := P + DATA.Size(P)
6 **return** $node$

3.4. Evaluation

expressions (prefixed with *Eval* and *Iter*) have an *Iterator()* method, which returns the evaluated next node, or null if all no more results are found. The *Iterator()* method of the *Axis* enumeration returns an iterator for the specified *Node*. *NodeTest.Matches()* returns true if the specified node complies with the test. A test may accept all nodes (*AnyKindTest*), nodes of a specific *Kind* (*KindTest*), or elements and attributes with a certain name (*NameTest*)[13]. If the test is successful, the predicates are evaluated.

We will now have a closer look on the individual expressions, starting bottom-up with the axis implementations. Both database (*DiskNode*) and constructed (*MemNode*) nodes offer particular implementations for all XPath axes: while the memory-based iterators are similar to conventional tree traversals, the database variants have been derived from the Staircase Join algorithms and, hence, are more interesting in this context.

Algorithm 25 lists the *Next()* methods of the iterators of 10 of the 12 XPath axes, which all can be implemented without considerable effort. As indicated in the last section, all nodes are traversed one by one. A simple integer (P) references the current pre value. null is returned if an axis will return no more nodes. Otherwise, P is updated, and a new *Node* instance is created and returned. For some axes, which do not return a self reference, the pre cursor needs to be initialized differently. As an example, in the prolog of the *Following.Next()* method, the descendants of the initial node are skipped; after that, the cursor is incremented by the node's attribute size ($asize$). All algorithms are optimal in the sense that only the relevant nodes are touched (in contrast, e.g., the $pre/post/level$ encoding requires a traversal of all descendants to find *child* nodes).

The two missing axes are *preceding* and *preceding-sibling*. As the nodes of the axes are to be returned in reverse document order (as is the case with the *ancestor* axes), and as no direct reference to left siblings is available in our encoding, a *NodeIterator* is used to cache the results in ascending order, and then return them in backward direction. Even so, only the nodes will be touched that contribute to the final result. To avoid caching, the database table can as well be traversed backwards, and all touched nodes can be matched against the axis. A reverse traversal is much slower, however, as many irrelevant nodes are touched (including attributes, which will never be addressed by the *preceding* axes). Next, usual prefetching strategies on hard disk are optimized for reading forward. As *preceding* and *following* axes are rarely used in practice, implementation details are skipped, and the reader is referred to the source code of BASEX [Grü10].

---

[13] The XQuery specification specifies more advanced tests for element, attribute and document nodes, which have been excluded from this overview.

On the next, higher level, the *IterStep* expression loops through all nodes that are returned by the axis iterator. Its *Next()* method has many similarities with the *Filter* variant, which has been presented in 3.4.1.3. Algorithm 26 will only yield valid results if at most one positional test is specified, which must additionally be placed as first predicate. Note that this limitation is not intrinsic to iterative processing; instead, it was introduced to simplify the presented pseudo-code. If a separate context position is managed and cached for each predicate, the algorithm will be able to process arbitrary positional predicates.

Algorithm 26 IterStep.Iterator.Next() : Node

Require:
    AXIS := XPath axis
    TEST := node test
    PREDS := filter predicates
    CONTEXT := query context
    ITERATOR := node iterator, generated from the AXIS and input node
    POS := 0 (current context position)
1 **loop**
2   POS := POS + 1
3   *node* := ITERATOR.Next()
4   **if** *node* = null **then**
5   **return** null
6   **else if** TEST.Matches(*node*) **then**
7   CONTEXT.VALUE := *node*
8   CONTEXT.POS := POS
9   **for** *pred* **in** PREDS **do**
10   **break if** the *truth value* of *pred* is false
11   **end for**
12   **return** *node* **if** all predicates tests were successful
13   **end if**
14 **end loop**

In contrast to the filter expression, the step iterator additionally performs the node test before the predicates are considered. Next, the context item and position is not reset, as this will be done once for all steps by the path expression.

Finally, Algorithm 27 shows the *Next()* method of the *IterPath*, which creates and triggers the axis step iterators and returns the results of the last step. The ITERATORS variable contains references to the step iterators, the first of which is initialized before the first call (the optional root expression is excluded from this algorithm; it is treated the same way as the axis steps). The original context value and position are cached before and

3.4. Evaluation

Algorithm 27 IterPath.Iterator.Next() : Node

Require:
    ITERATORS := iterator array
    CONTEXT := query context
    ITERATORS[0] = STEPS[0].Iterator()
    P := 0 (index on current iterator)

1   cache context value and position
2   **loop**
3      $node$:= ITERATORS[P].Next()
4   **if** $node$ = null **then**
5   P := P − 1
6   **break if** P < 0
7   **else if** p < #ITERATORS − 1 **then**
8   P := P + 1
9   CONTEXT.VALUE := $node$
10   ITERATORS[P] = STEPS[P].Iterator()
11   **else**
12   **break**
13   **end if**
14   **end loop**
15   restore context value and position
16   **return** $node$

---

restored after the evaluation. In the main loop, the next item is requested from the current iterator, which is referenced by P. If the iterator is exhausted, the next higher iterator is addressed by decrementing P. If the leftmost iterator (i.e., the first location step) returns null, the loop is canceled, as the location path will return no more results. Otherwise, if the current iterator is not the rightmost, P is incremented, the evaluated node is set as context node and the iterator of the next location step is initialized. If P points to the last location step, the evaluated node is returned as result.

3.4.2.3 Optimizations

The proposed framework offers room for numerous tweaks and improvements, both conceptual and technical, which will further speed up the evaluation of location paths. Some of the most important optimizations are sketched in the following. First of all, the *IterStep* algorithm is clearly suboptimal, regarding the evaluation of *positional predicates*:

- All nodes are iterated, even if a position test is specified that filters the resulting nodes to a small subset. In the example query `descendant::node()[1]`, the

3.4. Evaluation

iterator could be canceled after the first hit.

- Predicates using the `last()` function (which returns the last item of a sequence) are not supported, as the number of results is not known in advance. As the `last()` function will reduce the processed nodes to a single item, the conventional evaluation, which caches all nodes, is highly undesirable.

Algorithm 28 IterStep.Iterator.Next() : Node

Require: see Algorithm 26, plus:
    POSITION := position expression *(optional)*
    RETURNLAST := flag for returning the last node *(optional)*
    SKIP := `false`

1 **return** `null` **if** SKIP
2 $last := \text{null}$
3 **loop**
4   POS := POS + 1
5    $node :=$ ITERATOR.Next()
6   **if** $node = \text{null}$ **then**
7   SKIP := RETURNLAST
8   **return** $last$
9   **else if** TEST.Matches($node$) **then**
10   CONTEXT.VALUE := $node$
11   CONTEXT.POS := POS
12   **for** $pred$ **in** PREDS **do**
13   **break if** the *truth value* of $pred$ is `false`
14   **end for**
15   **if** all predicates tests were successful **then**
16   SKIP := POSITION.Skip(CONTEXT)
17   **return** $node$
18   **end if**
19   **if** RETURNLAST **then**
20       $last := node$
21   **end if**
22   **end if**
23 **end loop**

Algorithm 28 includes optimizations for the two requirements: RETURNLAST will be `true` if the step contains a single `last()` predicate, and POSITION will be assigned if the first predicate is an implementation-defined POSITION expression (see Section 3.5 for its definition). The SKIP flag indicates that the iterator will return no more results. It is set to `true` if the iterator is exhausted and the RETURNLAST flag is `true`, or if the *Skip()* method of the position expression returns `true` for the given context, indicating that

3.5. Summary

the context position has surpassed the given range. The *last* variable caches the last node that has been accepted by the node test. Note that both optimizations can also be applied to the filter iterator (Algorithm 21).

Another improvement can be applied to the evaluation of location paths: The iterative evaluation of path expressions is limited to descendant paths that follow certain patterns [HMV05]: *parent* steps may yield duplicate nodes, even if they are evaluated on ordered and duplicate-free node sets, as nodes can have the same parents. Still, the proposed *IterPath* method can be easily extended to also evaluate parent steps: Before a node is returned, it is cached by the iterator. If a cached node already exists, its node identity is compared with the new node. If both nodes have the same identity, the new node is ignored. This optimization is particularly helpful if a query is rewritten for index access, in which case child steps are inverted to parent steps.

Another simple yet effective optimization concerns the *instantiation* of new objects, which is an expensive operation in most programming languages. The proposed axis iterators continuously create new *DiskNode* objects, most of which will not contribute to the final result. This can be avoided by creating a single, initial node instance, which is updated with the current iterator values. If this node is accepted by a step expression, a copy of it is returned as result.

3.5 Summary

This section summarizes the optimizations and rewritings that have been applied to the most important XQuery expressions; we hope that they might serve as inspiration for other implementors of XQuery, and similar languages. The expression syntax is inspired by the W3C Recommendations, in which further details on the expressions can be looked up [BCF$^+$07, MMW07]). To save space, the following abbreviations are used for the summary of each expression:

- **S** contains the *semantics* of an expression.
- **P** describes operations in the *parsing* step that differ from the proposals in the specification (of course, all expression will continue to comply with the specification).
- **C** contains query *compilation* steps. If an expression is "returned", it will replace the original expression in the query plan.
- **I** includes information how an expression is rewritten for *index* access, and how costs will be estimated.

E refers to *evaluation*/runtime optimizations.

X adds examples to illustrate how some of the compilation steps work. Numbers have been added to the compilation steps and examples to show their relationship.

The following keywords are used as placeholders for returned expressions in the compilation step:

- **EMPTY** designates the empty item sequence ().
- **TRUE** and **FALSE** are equivalents for the boolean items `true` and `false`.

Some optimizations are skipped in this context, as they have already been described in the previous sections. For example, details on *constant folding* would be mostly redundant, as this optimization can be applied to nearly all operators. Next, some expressions will be introduced that have no equivalent in the specifications, as they result from compiling other expressions. Consequently, their proposed syntax and semantics is specific to our implementation.

ARITHMETIC: o_1 {+|-|*|div|idiv|mod} o_2 → item()?

 S The arithmetic operator is applied to the atomized operands. Besides numbers, also dates and durations can be computed and returned, according to the Operator Mapping of the specification.

 C1 **EMPTY** is returned if one operand will never yield results.

 E Evaluation of the second operand is skipped if the first yields an empty sequence.

 X1 `1 + (10 to 1)` → `()`

CONDITIONAL: `if(c) then` e_1 `else` e_2 → item()*

 S If the *effective boolean value* of condition c yields `true`, e_1 is evaluated. Otherwise, e_2 is evaluated.

 C1 If the condition is a value, the correct branch is selected and returned.

 C2 If both branches are identical, the condition is ignored and the identical result is returned. This optimization assumes that the condition causes no side-effects.

 C3 If the first branch is `true` and the second is `false`, the expression is replaced by a function `fn:boolean(c)`.

 C4 If the first branch is `false` and the second is `true`, the expression is replaced by a function `fn:not(c)`.

 C5 If the condition is enclosed by `fn:not(c)`, the function is removed and the branches are swapped.

 X1 `if(1) then local:run() else error()` → `local:run()`

3.5. Summary

   X2 `if(local:process()) then 'ok' else 'ok'` → `'ok'`
   X3 `if(tp:desc()) then true() else false()` → `boolean(tp:desc())`
   X5 `if(not(tp:desc())) then 0 else 1` → `if(tp:desc()) then 1 else 0`

EXCEPT: o_1 except o_2 → node()*

   S All nodes of the first evaluated operand are returned that are not contained in the second.
   P Consecutive `except` operators are parsed into one expression.
   C **EMPTY** is returned if the first operand yields an empty sequence. Other operands yielding empty sequences are removed. If one operand is left that yields sorted and duplicate-free nodes, this operand is returned.

FILTER: $e\,[p_1]\ldots[p_n]$ → item()*

   S The resulting items of an expression are filtered by one or more predicates.
   C1 If the expression will never return results, **EMPTY** is returned.
   C2 All predicate values yielding `true` are removed. If no predicates remain, the original expression is returned. **EMPTY** is returned if one of the predicates yields `false`.
   C3 Numeric predicates are rewritten to **POSITION** expressions.
   X1 `(//*[text() = 'not found in the index'])[1]` → `()`
   X2 `<xml/>[true()]['ok']` → `<xml/>`

FLWOR: (for…|let…)+ (where w)? (order by o)? return r → item()*

   S Values are iteratively mapped to variables, filtered, ordered, and returned.
   C1 The **WHERE** clause is rewritten to one or more predicates, which are attached to an innermost FOR clause; see 3.3.1.6 for details.
   C2 **LET** clauses and **FOR** clauses with one result are statically bound to their references.
   C3 If **WHERE** will always yield `true`, it is removed. **EMPTY** is returned if it always yields `false`.
   C4 If one **FOR** clause will never yield results, **EMPTY** is returned.
   C5 Declarations of statically bound variables are eliminated. If no variable declaration is left, the return expression is returned. If a **WHERE** clause is specified, a **CONDITIONAL** expression is returned.
   C6 Expressions with one **FOR/LET** clause, no **WHERE/ORDER** clause and a single variable reference in the **RETURN** clause are simplified.
   X1 `for $n in //Medium where $n/Type = 'DVD' return $n/Title`

3.5. Summary

```
   → for $n in //Medium[Type = 'DVD'] return $n/Title
X3 for $n in 1 to 10 where 3 < 2 return $n → ()
X4 for $n in () let $1 := (1,2,3) return ($n, $1) → ()
X5 let $1 := 1 where <x/> return $n → if(<x/>) then $1 else ()
X6 for $i in //item return $i → //item
```

FUNCTION CALL: $n(a_1, ..., a_n) \to \text{item}()^*$

- **S** The function named n is evaluated with the specified arguments $a_1, ..., a_n$.
- **C1** If all function arguments are values, and if the function result is a value, this value is returned.
- **C2** Functions that are never referenced at compile time, or have been inlined, will be eliminated.
- **X1** `declare function math:pi() { 3.14159265 }; math:pi() → 3.14159265`

GENERAL COMPARISON: $o_1 \{=|!=|<|<=|>=|>\} o_2 \to$ xs:boolean

- **S** All items of the evaluated operands are compared to each other, according to the Operator Mapping of the specification. **TRUE** is returned if one of the comparisons yields true.
- **C1** **FALSE** is returned if one operand will never yield results.
- **C2** Identical to the **VALUE COMPARISON**, just as **C3**, **C4**, and **C5**.
- **C5** Additionally, a **POSITION** expression is returned for a `fn:position()` function and a range expression.
- **C6** If possible, a **RANGE COMPARISON** expression is returned for numeric comparisons. This expression can be combined with other range tests more easily, or rewritten for range index access.
- **C7** A boolean flag SINGLE is set to indicate if all operands will yield single items.
- **I1** If possible, the operator is rewritten for index access; see 3.3.2.2 for details.
- **I2** If several expressions are specified as search terms, a **UNION** expression with multiple index operators will be returned. Index requests with zero results are ignored.
- **E** If the SINGLE flag was set to true, all operands will be directly evaluated to single items. Otherwise, **TRUE** is returned as soon as a comparison is positive (see 3.3.3 for more details on evaluating general comparisons).
- **X5** `address[position() = 1 to 5] → address[1...5]`
- **X6** `salary[text() > 1000] → salary[1000 < text() < ∞]`

INTERSECT: o_1 intersect $o_2 \to \text{node}()^*$

- **S** All nodes are returned that occur in all of the evaluated operands.

3.5. Summary

  P Consecutive `intersect` operators are parsed into one expression.
  C **EMPTY** is returned if one of the operands will never yields results.

LOGICAL AND: o_1 and o_2 → xs:boolean

  S The operands are evaluated to their *effective boolean values*. `true` is returned if all booleans are `true`. Otherwise, the result is `false`.

  P Consecutive and operators (o_1 and ... and o_n) are parsed into one expression. This flattens the operator tree and allows for an easier optimization.

  C1 All values yielding `true` are removed. If no operands remain, **TRUE** is returned. If one operand remains, it is returned as new expression. If this operand yields no boolean value, it is wrapped in a `fn:boolean()` function. **FALSE** is returned if at least one of the values yields `false`.

  C2 Multiple **POSITION** expressions are merged. If the merged position range will never yield `true`, **FALSE** is returned.

  C3 Multiple **RANGE COMPARISON** expressions are merged. If the merged expression will result in an impossible range, **FALSE** is returned.

  I1 If all operands can benefit from an index, an **INTERSECT** expression will be returned, containing all operands rewritten for index access.

  I2 Costs for index access are summarized. All index operations will be sorted by their costs in an ascending order to evaluate the cheapest index operation first. If one index operation will yield zero hits, **EMPTY** is returned.

  E **FALSE** is returned as soon as one operand yields `false`.

  X1 `1 and 'two' and xs:boolean(true())` → `true`
  X2 `node[position() >= 1 and position() <= 10]` → `node[1...10]`
  X3 `//person[@income >= 1000 and @income < 5000]` →
       `//person[1000 <= @income < 5000]`

LOGICAL OR: o_1 or o_2 → xs:boolean

  S The operands are evaluated to their *effective boolean values*. `false` is returned if all booleans are `false`. Otherwise, `true` is returned.

  P Same as **LOGICAL AND**: consecutive or operators are parsed into one expression.

  C1 In analogy to **AND**: All values yielding `false` are removed. If no operands remain, **FALSE** is returned. If one operand remains, it is returned as new expression. If this operand yields no boolean value, it is wrapped in a `fn:boolean()` function. **TRUE** is returned if at least one of the values yields `true`.

  C2 Multiple **GENERAL COMPARISON** expressions are merged if their left operand is identical. Expressions of this kind can better be rewritten for index access.

3.5. Summary

I1 If all operands can benefit from an index, an **UNION** expression will be returned, containing all operands rewritten for index access.

I2 Costs for index access are summarized. If a single index operation will yield zero hits, it is ignored. If no index operation will yield any hits, **EMPTY** is returned.

E `true` is returned as soon as one operand yields `true`.

X2 `//node[text() = 'A' or text() = 'B']` → `//node[text() = ('A', 'B')]`

NODE COMPARISON: o_1 {`<<`|`is`|`>>`} o_2 → xs:boolean?

S The operands are evaluated to nodes and compared in terms of their node identity.

C **EMPTY** is returned if one operand will never yield results.

E Evaluation of the second operand is skipped if the first yields an empty sequence.

X `//text() is //text()/text()` → `()`

POSITION: $min \ldots max$ → xs:boolean

S This implementation specific expression is a normalized representation of positional predicates, containing a minimum and maximum integer value. `true` is returned if the current context position lies within the given range. An additional *Skip()* method checks if the context position surpasses the range.

RANGE: o_1 `to` o_2 → xs:integer*

S A sequence of consecutive integers is created, ranging from o_1 to o_2. Range expressions will never be pre-evaluated if the result would include more than one integer; instead, light-weight iterators are created at runtime.

C1 If either operand will never yield values, or if the first operand yields an integer larger than the second, **EMPTY** is returned.

C2 If both operands yield the same integers, that integer is returned.

X1 `10 to 1` → `()`

X2 `1 to 1` → `1`

RANGE COMPARISON: min {`<`|`<=`} o {`<`|`<=`} max: xs:boolean

S Some comparisons are rewritten into this implementation specific expression, which contains an operand to be evaluated and a minimum and maximum double value. `true` is returned if expression e lies within the given range.

I1 The operator is rewritten for index access, similar to step **I1** of the **GENERAL COMPARISON**.

I2 In accordance with the database statistics, if possible, the minimum and maximum values are reduced for the tested text or attribute name.

3.5. Summary

I3 20% of the number of database nodes is set as costs to indicate that sequential access might be faster if several index operations are to be performed.

TYPESWITCH: `typeswitch (c) ({case t|default} return e)+` → `item()*`

- **S** Depending on the type of expression c, one of the specified branches is evaluated and returned. The syntax shown above is simplified.
- **C1** If the type of the condition is known due to static typing, the correct branch is selected and returned.
- **C2** If all conditions specify the same result, the condition is ignored and the result is returned. This optimization assumes that the condition causes no side-effects.
- **X1** `typeswitch(xs:int('1')) case xs:int return 2 default return 3` → `2`
- **X2** `typeswitch('a') case xs:string return () default return ()` → `()`

UNION: o_1 `union` o_2 → `node()*`

- **S** All nodes are returned that occur in either of the evaluated operands.
- **P** Consecutive `union` operators are parsed into one expression.
- **C** All operands yielding empty sequences are removed. If no operand is left, **EMPTY** is returned. If one operand is left that yields sorted and duplicate-free nodes, it is returned as new expression.

VALUE COMPARISON: o_1 `(eq|ne|lt|le|ge|gt)` o_2 → `xs:boolean?`

- **S** The operands are evaluated to items and compared to each other, according to the Operator Mapping of the specification.
- **C1** **EMPTY** is returned if one operand will never yield results.
- **C2** If values and non-values are specified as operands, the expression is normalized: the value is specified as second operand, and the operator is inversed.
- **C3** `text()` steps are added to location paths if database meta data indicates that the result will be identical. Atomization will be cheaper, and expressions can be better rewritten for index access (see Section 3.3.2).
- **C4** if possible, `fn:count()` functions are rewritten to `fn:empty()` or `fn:exist()`. The latter functions may be cheaper, as only the first resulting item need to be touched.
- **C5** if possible, `fn:position()` functions are rewritten to an implementation specific **POSITION** expression.
- **E** Evaluation of the second operand is skipped if the first yields an empty sequence.
- **X2** `node[123 lt text()]` → `node[text() gt 123]`
- **X3** `city[name eq 'Roma']` → `city[name/text() eq 'Roma']`
- **X4** `count(//item) gt 0 and count(//person) eq 0`

→ `exists(//item) and empty(//person)`
X5 `address[position() le 10]` → `address[1...10]`

VARIABLE REFERENCE: v → item()*

- **S** The expression, which is bound to v, is evaluated and returned.
- **C1** If variables are global, specify a fragment, or contain a function call, they will be pre-evaluated by the compiler if they are referenced for the first time.
- **C2** Variables that are never referenced at compile time will be eliminated.
- **X2** `declare variable $x := doc('input.xml'); <xml/>` → `<xml/>`

3.6 Examples

3.6.1 Index Access

This section contains supplementary example queries along with the expression trees, both in their original and compiled form. As will be seen, most optimizes plans are more compact than the original ones.

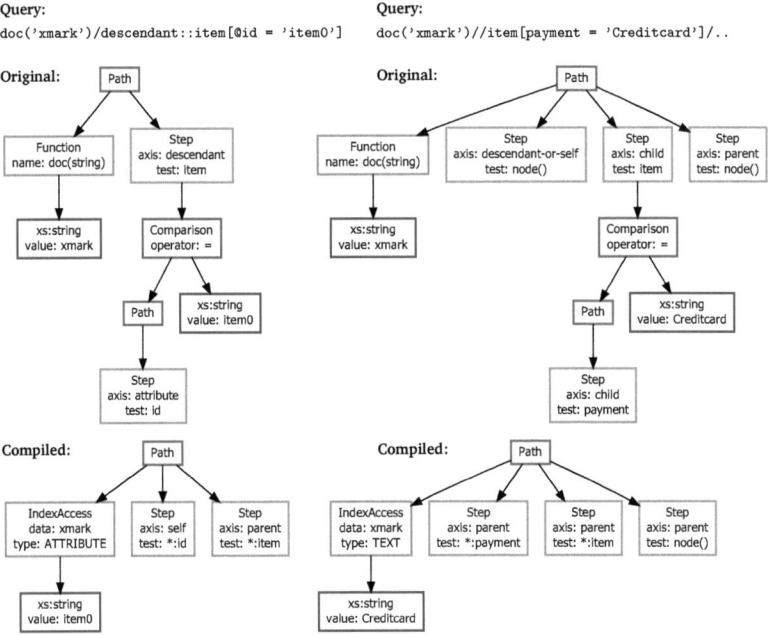

Figure 3.8: Query 1 & 2: Path expressions with equality comparison

Figure 3.8 contains two queries that are rewritten for index access. In the first query, the doc() is pre-evaluated to get access to the database meta information. Next, the comparison operator is rewritten for index access, the predicate is rewritten to an inverted path. Two additional, intermediate optimizations are performed in the second query, which cannot be seen in the final plan: The *descendant-or-self* and *child* steps are merged to a single *descendant* step. Next, based on the information given in the database statistics, the Comparison operator attaches a `text()` to the `payment` step to indicate the index rewriter that this step has only leaf nodes.

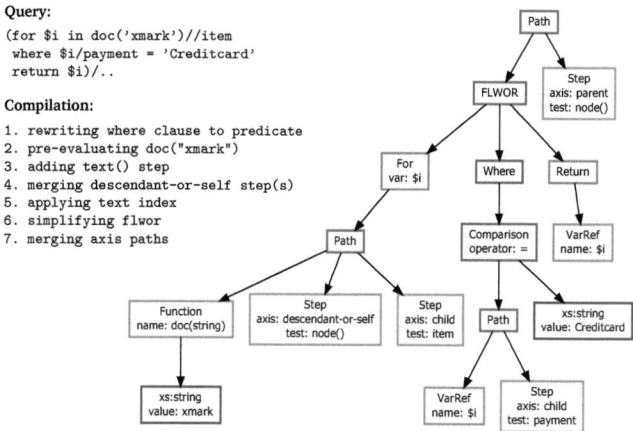

Figure 3.9: Query 3: FLWOR expression with equality comparison

Another query is shown in Figure 3.9, which yields the same optimized plan as Query 2. The query is written as a FLWOR expression; as such, the compiler first attaches the WHERE clause as predicate to the location step of the FOR clause. After all other optimizations have been performed, the FLWOR expression is eliminated, and the resulting index path is merged with the suffixed parent step.

3.6.2 XMark

The following plans depict some of the XMark Benchmark queries [SWK⁺02] (see Section 4.2.2.3 for a list of all queries). In Figure 3.10, XMark Query 1 is depicted, which bears some similarities with the previous expressions. The outer FLWOR expression, which only contains a LET clause defining the input document, is eliminated, and the location path of the inner FOR clause is rewritten to an index access. Note that the index access smoothly integrates in the remaining FLWOR expression: each index result is iteratively bound to the variable of the FOR clause.

3.6. Examples

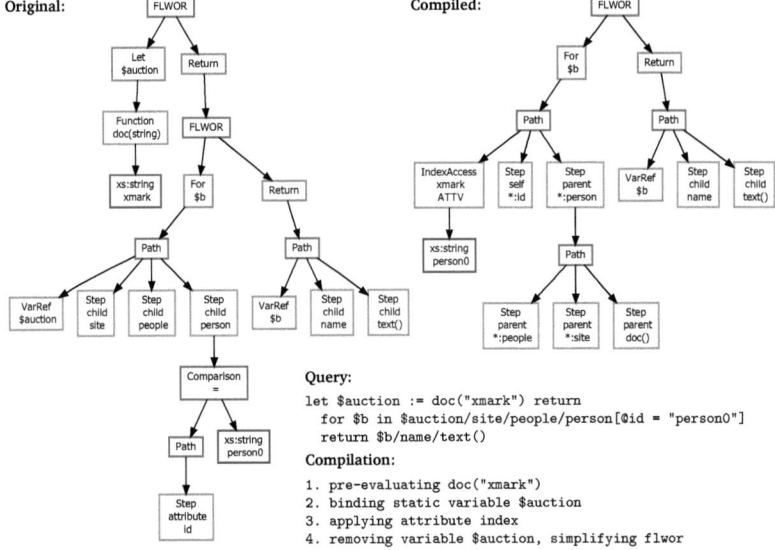

Figure 3.10: XMark Query 1: Original and optimized query plan

Figure 3.11 is presented in XMark Query 7, which is similar to the query shown in 3.3.1.3, as it can be completely pre-evaluated at compile time. The three fn:count() functions yield the number of nodes of a sub-tree of the document. The most important compilation steps are as follows:

Many of the optimizations in this query are due to the path summary: after the document reference has been pre-evaluated (1) and the $auction variable has been statically bound to its references (2), the expression of the FOR clause is bound to the variable $p (3): the path summary indicates that the document only contains one site element, which means that variable $p will only return one single value and, hence, can be statically bound. Next, the *descendant-or-self* and *child* steps are rewritten to a simple *descendant* step (4), and the path summary is once more accessed to compute the number of elements for the resulting path /child::site/descendant::description (5). The same steps are performed for the remaining paths, and the number of final results is calculated by pre-evaluating the calculation operators.

3.6. Examples

Compilation:
1. pre-evaluating doc("xmark")
2. binding static variable $auction
3. binding static variable $p
4. merging descendant-or-self step
5. pre-evaluating count(...)
6. merging descendant-or-self step
7. pre-evaluating count(...)
8. pre-evaluating 45 + 22
9. merging descendant-or-self step
10. pre-evaluating count(...)
11. pre-evaluating 67 + 25
12. removing variable $p
13. simplifying flwor
14. removing variable $auction
15. simplifying flwor

Query:
```
let $auction := doc('xmark') return
  for $p in $auction/site return
    count($p//description) +
    count($p//annotation) +
    count($p//emailaddress)
```

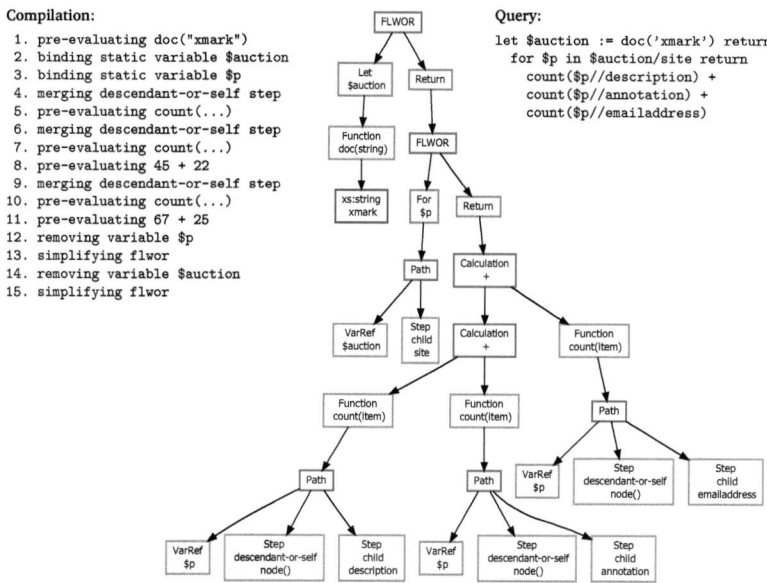

Figure 3.11: XMark Query 7: Original query plan

XMark queries 8-12 contain nested loops and yield quadratic costs if they are evaluated without optimizations. XMark Query 9 is presented in more detail: it includes six FLWOR expressions, only three of which remain after the query has been compiled: First of all, the input document is pre-evaluated and statically bound to all its references. Next, the expressions of the LET variables $ca and $ei are bound. After the first WHERE clause has been converted to a predicate, and the arguments of the comparison operator have been swapped, the first path can be rewritten for index access. Similar optimizations are applied to the second WHERE clause and equality comparison, resulting in a simplification of the embracing FLWOR expression. Finally, after the removal of the obsolete variable declarations, two other FLWOR expressions are eliminated. As a result, the costs for the query are decreased from $\mathcal{O}(n^2)$ to $\mathcal{O}(n * \log n)$, provided that the applied indexes yield results in logarithmic time.

An additional XMark Query 21 has been added to this section, which is not part of the benchmark, but which demonstrates the flexibility of the rewriting mechanism for the WHERE clause: The query depicted in Figure 3.13 comprises one FLWOR expression

103

3.6. Examples

Compilation:
1. pre-evaluating doc("xmark")
2. binding static variable $auction
3. binding static variable $ca
4. binding static variable $ei
5. rewriting where clause
6. swapped: buyer/@person = $p/@id
7. applying attribute index
8. rewriting where clause
9. swapped: @id = $t/itemref/@item
10. applying attribute index
11. simplifying flwor
12. removing variable $ei
13. removing variable $ca
14. simplifying flwor
15. removing variable $auction
16. simplifying flwor

Query:
```
let $auction := doc("xmark") return
let $ca := $auction/site/closed_auctions/
   closed_auction return
let $ei :=
   $auction/site/regions/europe/item
for $p in $auction/site/people/person
let $a :=
   for $t in $ca
   where $p/@id = $t/buyer/@person
   return
      let $n := for $t2 in $ei
                where $t/itemref/@item = $t2/@id
                return $t2
      return <item>{$n/name/text()}</item>
return <person name="{$p/name/text()}">{ $a }</person>
```

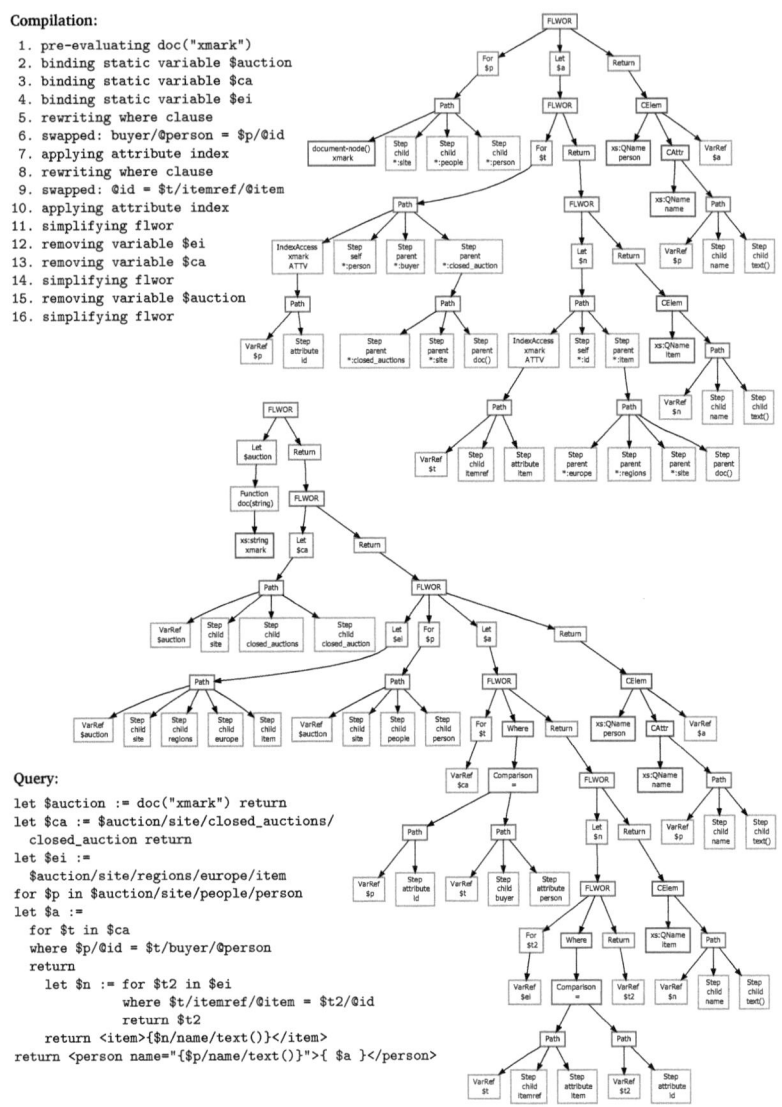

Figure 3.12: XMark Query 9: Optimized/original query plan (top/bottom)

3.6. Examples

with three FOR clauses, one of them including two range comparisons, and a WHERE clause with two equality comparisons. First, the range operators are first converted to an implementation specific Range Comparison expression, and the two equality tests are attached to the corresponding location paths. Next, all comparisons are rewritten to first access the appropriate index structure. Based on the database statistics, the minimum and maximum values of the range index access are modified in order to not exceed the limits of the actual data.

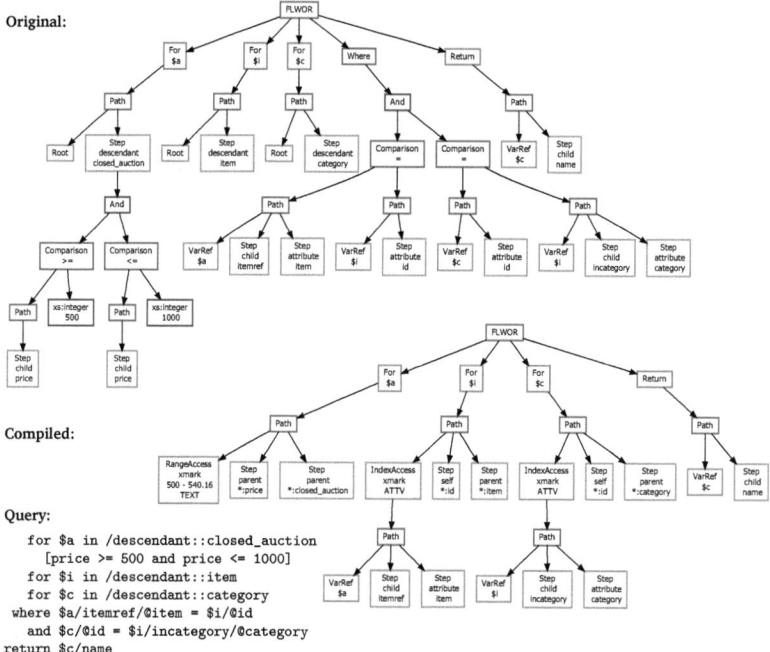

Query:
```
for $a in /descendant::closed_auction
         [price >= 500 and price <= 1000]
for $i in /descendant::item
for $c in /descendant::category
where $a/itemref/@item = $i/@id
  and $c/@id = $i/incategory/@category
return $c/name
```

Figure 3.13: (Inofficial) XMark Query 21: Optimized/original query plan

4 Performance

If one parses the database publications, it seems groundbreaking how many "most efficient" and "best" algorithms and techniques have been designed and implemented over the last 30 years. The same observation accounts for newer performance results on XML and XQuery, let alone the advertisements of commercial products. Summarizing, it is no secret that everyone wants to be Number One, and, at the same time, it is well-known that each scientific approach and code project excels in different areas. Accordingly, we do know that we are Number One as well, and we could easily enough limit our performance tests to a "most relevant" subset of queries to prove this claim. –Instead, we want to point out that we have not come across any XQuery processor or database that will beat all others, but there are surely some that focus on performance, while others put more efforts into compliance or a rich feature list. Hence, this observation is meant as an introductory warning, and to avoid that the presented performance results are interpreted as the only relevant dimensions.

The performance of BASEX, our native XML database and XQuery processor that embraces all the techniques listed in the previous two chapters, is central to this chapter. First of all, we will benchmark the performance of our *storage* unit and measure the time needed to build new database instances and index structures. The results will be compared with some other Open Source XML databases. Second, we will focus on its *query* capabilities, and compare BASEX with additional XQuery processors. Finally, we will present some *statistics* on very large database instances that have been built with our system.

ID	CPU	RAM	Hard disk	OS	Bits
Dual	Intel Dual Core T7300 2.0 GHz	2 GB	80 GB	Windows XP SP3	32
Xeon	Intel Xeon 2.33 GHz	32 GB	450 GB	Linux 2.6.27 (Suse 10.2)	64
AMD	AMD Opteron 2.2 GHz	16 GB	400 GB	Linux 2.6.13 (Suse 10.0)	64

Table 4.1: Hardware architectures used for testing

All tests in this section have been performed with Version 6.3 of BASEX. Three different hardware architectures have been used for testing, which are shown in Table 4.1, and which will from now on be addressed by their IDs *Xeon*, *Dual*, and *AMD*.

4.1 Storage

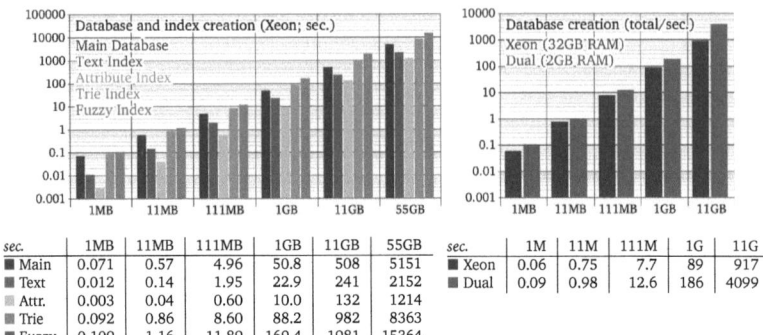

Figure 4.1: Database creation of XMark instances with BASEX. Left: single times for database and index creation, right: total time on different architectures

Figure 4.1 demonstrates the performance results for building databases from six XMark instances ([SWK+02], see also 4.2.2). The left diagram was performed on the *Xeon* machine with 32GB RAM. It lists times for creating the database and the four index structures. Text and attribute indexing is very fast, whereas the full-text indexes, which are optional and interchangeable, take approximately the same time as is needed for building the database, as all text nodes need to be tokenized and normalized. The right diagram compares build times measured on the two test architectures with a different amount of RAM; this time, the results include the creation of the text and attribute indexes, which are activated by default. It can be observed that more RAM speeds up the creation of large databases. The memory consumption for creating the database table is low for all instances, as all data is directly written to disk: instead, it is the index creation process that takes up a lot of memory. The existing index builders have been optimized to dynamically adapt to the available memory (see 2.6.3.3 for details). As a result, also the 1GB and 11GB document instances can be successfully built with 2GB RAM. 32GB RAM is needed, however, to build indexes for the 55GB instance, as the intermediate data structures, which are created by the index builder, are too large to fit into main memory.

Obviously, the time for building index structures is strongly dependent on the input data. If a document contains many attributes, the costs for building the attribute index might equal or surpass the text index. Figure 4.2 shows the numerically sorted timing results

4.1. Storage

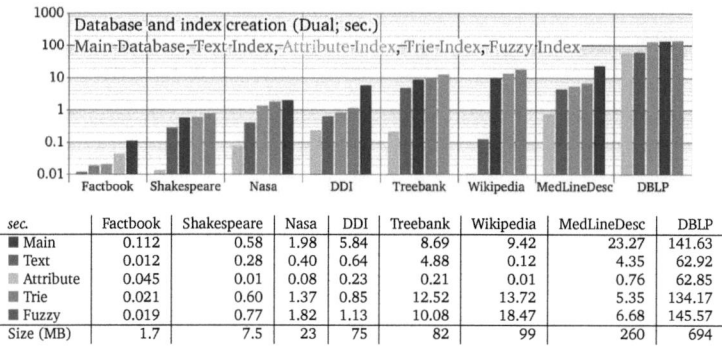

Figure 4.2: Database creation of various smaller XML instances (Sources: Table 4.5)

for some smaller documents. Attribute indexing is comparatively time consuming for the Factbook, while the Shakespeare and Treebank is predominated by text nodes. The Wikipedia instance has just a few, but very long text nodes; consequently, most time is spent for creating the full-text indexes.

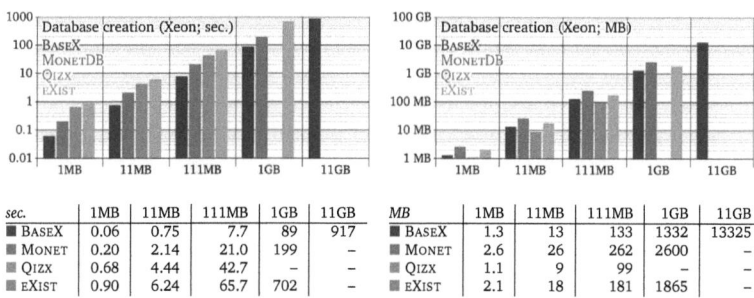

Figure 4.3: XMark documents: build times and database sizes

In Figure 4.3, BaseX is compared with some other Open Source XML engines. Commercial systems have been tested as well, but were omitted in the results due to legal restrictions. The first chart depicts the times that are needed to build XMark database instances, using the engines' default configurations, and the second chart summarizes the database size on disk. All engines have been sorted by their processing speed:

- BaseX is clearly the fastest database builder, processing an average of 12 MB/sec.

4.1. Storage

for both creating the database and the text and attributes indexes. Moreover, it was the only system that allowed us to create a database instance for the 11GB instance. The complete database size is around 120% of the original document size. The throughput rate is reduced to appr. 5.8 MB/sec. if full-text indexing is included.

- Next comes MONETDB 4.38.5 with a throughput rate of 5.2 MB/sec. for building the plain database. The resulting database is 260% of the original size. The largest document we managed to shred with the latest version was 1 GB; earlier versions of MONETDB, however, are known to have supported instances of up to 11 GB (see e.g. [GHK+06]).

- QIZX 4.0 is placed third, parsing 2.3 MB/sec. The resulting database includes all index structures and is only appr. 90% of the input size. Only three XMark instances could have been built, as the free version of the software is limited to documents of less than 1 GB.

- EXIST 1.4.0 comes last with 1.6 MB/sec. and a database size of 160% of the original input size.

The unrivaled build performance of BASEX can be attributed to the flat table representation, which is an ideal candidate for sequential storage, and the compactification of the table attributes, which reduces the amount of data to be written. As a result, most of the build time is spent for parsing the XML input document and reading the data from disk. Next, as XML attributes are inlined in the main table, the organization of additional data structures is reduced. The inlining of integers contributes to a smaller database size. Presumably, BASEX yields better results than MONETDB as all storage patterns have been optimized for XML from the beginning; for example, the values of the $size$ property (which specify the number of descendants of a node and thus cannot be written in the first run) are cached and sequentially stored in a second run. This is faster than writing each value at the corresponding position once it has been evaluated (see 2.5.1 for a reminder). Next, MONETDB is column-based, storing each attribute separately, whereas BASEX holds all values in one compactified tuple, which is comparable to a single attribute.

Figure 4.4 opposes the *bulk* and *incremental* creation of database items. In BASEX, XML sources can be specified as initial database input via the CREATE DB statement (Query 3). Alternatively, documents and collections can be added in a second step with the ADD statement (Query 1 and 2). Obviously, Query 3 is performed fastest, as all documents

4.2. Querying

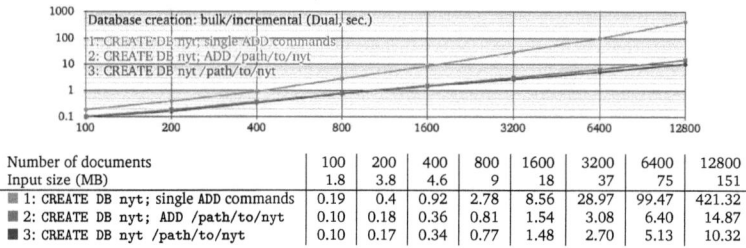

Number of documents	100	200	400	800	1600	3200	6400	12800
Input size (MB)	1.8	3.8	4.6	9	18	37	75	151
■ 1: `CREATE DB nyt`; single `ADD` commands	0.19	0.4	0.92	2.78	8.56	28.97	99.47	421.32
■ 2: `CREATE DB nyt; ADD /path/to/nyt`	0.10	0.18	0.36	0.81	1.54	3.08	6.40	14.87
■ 3: `CREATE DB nyt /path/to/nyt`	0.10	0.17	0.34	0.77	1.48	2.70	5.13	10.32

Figure 4.4: Bulk vs. incremental database creation (NEWYORKTIMES documents)

are added in a single run. In Query 2, all documents are added to the empty database in a second run, which nearly takes the same time, as the `ADD` statement triggers one single commit. Accordingly, Query 1 performs worst of all, as all documents are inserted one after another, leading to a repeated update of all database meta information. The insertion time grows quadratically as internal meta data of the database is updated after each single `ADD` operation.

4.2 Querying

In the following, BASEX will be compared with some more Open Source XQuery processors. Table 4.2 lists all implementations in question, along with their version, programming language, and the command line call that was used for testing. Due to limited space, the project names will often be exchanged with the IDs, shown in the first column:

ID	Project	Version	Lang.	Command line call
BA	BASEX	6.3	Java	`java -cp basex-6.3.jar org.basex.BaseX query.xq`
SA	SAXON-HE	9.2.0.7	Java	`java -cp saxon9he.jar net.sf.saxon.Query query.xq`
QI	QIZX	4.0	Java	`java -cp resolver.jar;qizx.jar com.qizx.apps.QizxCLI query.xq`
ZO	ZORBA	1.4	C++	`zorba.exe -f -q query.xq`
MX	MXQUERY	0.6	Java	`java -jar mxquery.jar -f query.xq`
BC	BASEX-C	6.3	Java	`java -cp basex-6.3.jar org.basex.BaseXClient query.xq`
MO	MONETDB	4.38.5	C++	`mclient.exe -lx query.xq`
EX	EXIST	1.4.0	Java	`curl http://localhost:8080/exist/rest/db -X post -T query.xml`

Table 4.2: Compared XQuery processors (standalone, client-/server architecture)

BASEX was tested both in the standalone and the client/server version (termed BASEX-C). Similar to EXIST and MONETDB, which are both based on a server architecture, client calls will usually be executed faster, as they benefit from shorter startup times and runtime optimizations of the server instance. The POST method of the REST interface

4.2. Querying

was used to communicate with EXIST, for which the respective query was wrapped into an XML fragment. All query results are serialized to temporary files.

Most processors offer numerous options to tweak specific queries. We decided to run all implementations with the default settings, as a fair optimization would require expert knowledge on each single project. Moreover, we believe that most users will start off with the default setup before going any further. Next, some implementations (including BASEX) generate optional timing output for each processing step, such as parsing, compilation, evaluation, or serialization. This information was ignored, and the total runtime was measured instead, as the analyzed projects embrace a too heterogeneous architecture to be reasonably compared in more depth:

- If an implementation processes queries in an iterative manner, the *evaluation* and *serialization* phase usually fall together, as the query will not be evaluated before the first result item is output.

- Some processors opt to completely evaluate simple queries in the *compilation* phase, whereas others will interpret the complete query, or compile parts of it just-in-time, i.e., in the *evaluation* phase.

- Last but not least, not all processors offer enough timing information to allow fair comparisons, or the output timing results differ too much from the total processing time.

The total runtime of the listed query processors is influenced by additional aspects: Some overhead is generated for initializing the program code, which sometimes exceeds the time for evaluating the actual query. This is particularly the case for Java programs, which depend on the initialization of the Virtual Machine, and which perform much faster after a longer runtime (as can be observed in the client version of BASEX). Finally, some additional time is needed for launching and terminating the code and measuring the performance.

sec.	BASEX	SAXON	QIZX	ZORBA	MXQUERY	BASEX-C	MONETDB	EXIST
min	0.252	0.562	0.308	0.143	0.253	0.202	0.057	0.049
med	0.263	0.562	0.312	0.148	0.261	0.211	0.062	0.055
max	0.270	0.624	0.375	0.157	0.270	0.217	0.065	0.068

Table 4.3: Usual runtimes for evaluating an empty sequence (15 runs)

All tests in this section were performed on the *Dual* system. The Linux `time` command was used to measure the *elapsed real time* between program invocation and termination. To get rid of the constant overhead for running the processors, the *median* of several runs

4.2. Querying

for evaluating an empty sequence () was measured (see Table 4.3), and was subtracted from the median of the actual performance result. The median was preferred over other values, such as the minimum value or the arithmetic mean, in order to suppress the influence of outliers, which are more common on command line than in tighter test settings. All tests were run 15 times. Consequently, most final results benefit from caching behavior of the operating system (the performed cold cache tests turned out to be too irreproducible to be further pursued in this work). A timeout of 5 minutes was used in all tests.

4.2.1 XQuery

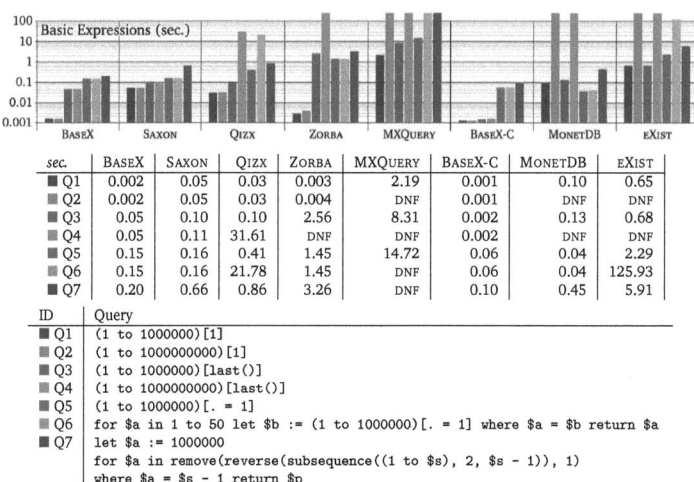

sec.	BaseX	Saxon	Qizx	Zorba	MXQuery	BaseX-C	MonetDB	eXist
■ Q1	0.002	0.05	0.03	0.003	2.19	0.001	0.10	0.65
■ Q2	0.002	0.05	0.03	0.004	DNF	0.001	DNF	DNF
■ Q3	0.05	0.10	0.10	2.56	8.31	0.002	0.13	0.68
■ Q4	0.05	0.11	31.61	DNF	DNF	0.002	DNF	DNF
■ Q5	0.15	0.16	0.41	1.45	14.72	0.06	0.04	2.29
■ Q6	0.15	0.16	21.78	1.45	DNF	0.06	0.04	125.93
■ Q7	0.20	0.66	0.86	3.26	DNF	0.10	0.45	5.91

ID	Query
■ Q1	(1 to 1000000)[1]
■ Q2	(1 to 1000000000)[1]
■ Q3	(1 to 1000000)[last()]
■ Q4	(1 to 1000000000)[last()]
■ Q5	(1 to 1000000)[. = 1]
■ Q6	for $a in 1 to 50 let $b := (1 to 1000000)[. = 1] where $a = $b return $a
■ Q7	let $a := 1000000 for $a in remove(reverse(subsequence((1 to $s), 2, $s - 1)), 1) where $a = $s - 1 return $p

Figure 4.5: Basic XQuery expressions: comparison of different processors.
DNF: did not finish within 5 min.

First, we will have a look at some basic XQuery expressions, which do not depend on XML resources. The seven queries presented in Figure 4.5 have been chosen to demonstrate the positive effects of performing static query optimizations, using the iterative concept, and accessing items via offsets. As was announced in the last paragraph, the time for evaluating an empty sequence was subtracted from the performance results. All queries return a single integer. This way, side effects were minimized, which are caused by the serialization of the results.

113

4.2. Querying

- Query *Q1* and *Q2* return the first value of a range of integers. 4 of the 7 engines evaluated both queries in the same amount of time. This reveals two things: First, the queries are evaluated in an iterative manner, as no time is spent for materializing the range expression. Second, processing is terminated after the first item, respectively, the relevant item is directly requested. In contrast, the other 3 engines either failed due to a lack of main memory, or did not terminate in the given time frame.

- In Query *Q3* and *Q4*, the last item of a range expression is returned. 2 engines (BASEX and SAXON) needed the same time for both queries, which indicates that the last item was directly requested. In QIZX, which also managed to return the results in the given time, the query was iteratively processed, leading to a longer execution time for the second query.

- One million integers are iterated by the filter expression in Query *Q5*, and the first item (i.e., the item that matches the general comparison with the integer 1) is chosen as result. MONETDB performs best here, most probably due to its simplified type system and column-based processing, whereas most other implementations create temporary objects for the integers. However, an error is raised by MONETDB if an item of another type is added to the iterated sequence.

- Query *Q6* includes the filter expression from Query *Q5* in the inner LET clause. This expression is evaluated 50 times by QIZX, MXQUERY, and EXIST. The timing of the other 4 engines shows that the LET clause is only computed once; this indicates that the result is either cached at runtime, or the LET clause is moved out of the FLWOR expression, as done in BASEX.

- The FOR clause in Query *Q7* specifies three sequence functions, which are wrapped around a range expression, specified by the outer LET clause. This time, BASEX managed to outpace the other engines: the evaluation time is nearly the same as for Query *Q5* and *Q6*, as the iterative processing and the direct access to values returned by the `subsequence()` function ensures that no values need to be cached (see 3.4.1).

As a follow-up, we have tested some advanced XQuery expressions, which are presented in Figure 4.6, along with the tabular and visual results. The first three queries contain recursive functions, while the fourth makes intensive use of sequence offsets. This time, not all implementations managed to parse or evaluate the selected queries; MONETDB even failed to compile any of them. The results indicate that 3 of the 7 processors

4.2. Querying

evaluated all four queries and did not exceed the given time frame. BaseX and Saxon yielded the best average runtime among the tested implementations; the client version of BaseX (which should only be compared to eXist) delivered much better results for all queries.

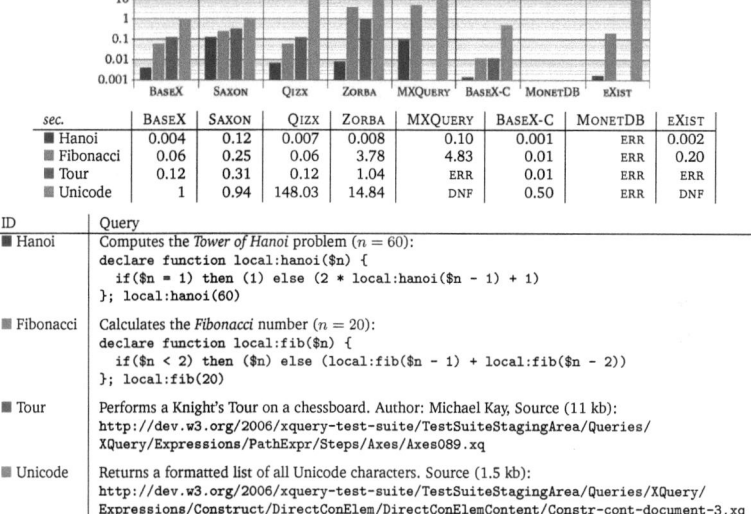

sec.	BaseX	Saxon	Qizx	Zorba	MXQuery	BaseX-C	MonetDB	eXist
■ Hanoi	0.004	0.12	0.007	0.008	0.10	0.001	ERR	0.002
■ Fibonacci	0.06	0.25	0.06	3.78	4.83	0.01	ERR	0.20
■ Tour	0.12	0.31	0.12	1.04	ERR	0.01	ERR	ERR
■ Unicode	1	0.94	148.03	14.84	DNF	0.50	ERR	DNF

ID	Query

■ Hanoi	Computes the *Tower of Hanoi* problem ($n = 60$):
	`declare function local:hanoi($n) {`
	`  if($n = 1) then (1) else (2 * local:hanoi($n - 1) + 1)`
	`}; local:hanoi(60)`

■ Fibonacci	Calculates the *Fibonacci* number ($n = 20$):
	`declare function local:fib($n) {`
	`  if($n < 2) then ($n) else (local:fib($n - 1) + local:fib($n - 2))`
	`}; local:fib(20)`

■ Tour	Performs a Knight's Tour on a chessboard. Author: Michael Kay, Source (11 kb): http://dev.w3.org/2006/xquery-test-suite/TestSuiteStagingArea/Queries/ XQuery/Expressions/PathExpr/Steps/Axes/Axes089.xq
■ Unicode	Returns a formatted list of all Unicode characters. Source (1.5 kb): http://dev.w3.org/2006/xquery-test-suite/TestSuiteStagingArea/Queries/XQuery/ Expressions/Construct/DirectConElem/DirectConElemContent/Constr-cont-document-3.xq

Figure 4.6: Advanced XQuery expressions: comparison of different processors. ERR: could not be evaluated, DNF: did not finish within 5 min.

- The first query represents a simple recursive function. It computes the *Tower of Hanoi* problem for a given number n. As the number of recursive calls is linear, this query is evaluated quickly by most implementations.

- The second function for computing the *Fibonacci* number contains two function calls to itself and, hence, causes exponential costs. The Java implementations, headed by BaseX and Qizx, yielded the best results.

- Several recursive user functions are specified by the third query, computing a solution for the Knight's Tour problem. Due to its complexity, 3 of the 7 engines failed to return a solution, while the others delivered competitive times. Again, BaseX and Qizx win the race (however, the commercial version of Saxon, which has not

115

4.2. Querying

been tested in this scope, is known to yield good results on this query).

- The last query outputs a formatted list of all Unicode characters. All valid codepoints are defined in a sequence, which is accessed via offsets. The performance results indicate that SAXON, and possibly ZORBA, offer similar optimizations to BASEX, which directly accesses the addressed sequence items (as has been described in detail in 3.3.3.1).

4.2.2 XMark

XMark is the de facto reference XQuery benchmark in scientific publications [SWK+02]. Some of the queries and their BASEX expression trees have already been demonstrated in 3.6.2. First, we will analyze the time needed for building main-memory instances of XMark document instances. Next, we will compare the query times and demonstrate the scalability of BASEX. Last, based on the benchmark, we will sketch how the performance of our query architecture has improved version by version.

4.2.2.1 Main Memory Processing

XMLGEN is used to create XML documents of arbitrary size, which then serve as input for the XMark queries[1]. In the first test, we measured the time and footprint for processing a 111MB document in main memory. To guarantee that the document is actually opened, and to minimize the overhead for query processing, the doc() function was used, followed by a child step on comment nodes (another attempt to wrap doc() with a count() function did not suffice, as the query was pre-evaluated by some processors in constant time).

Figure 4.7 shows the times needed for evaluating the query (minus the usual overhead for an empty sequence), and the occupied memory. Both charts are numerically sorted, placing the best results first. For Java implementations, the available memory has been limited by setting the -Xmx flag. The memory consumption for the other engines was approximated over several runs and document instances of different sizes. As the results show, QIZX offers the fastest document builder, followed by the server-based BASEX and EXIST engines. The standalone version of BASEX is comparatively slow, as the same

---

[1]Source: http://www.xml-benchmark.org

4.2. Querying

representation is used for disk-based database instances and document instances in main memory (see 2.5.3).

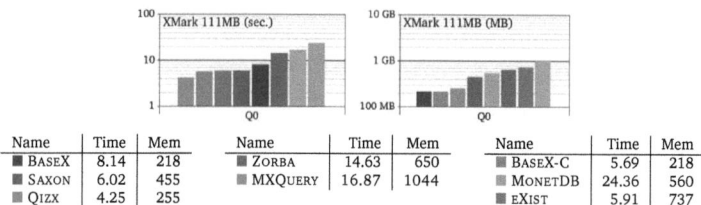

Figure 4.7: Opening a 111MB XMark document in main memory

In compensation, the identical storage structure pays off in terms of memory footprint, which is much lower than with most other implementations: except for QIZX, all processors need at least twice the space of BASEX, and four to ten times the memory of the original document. Next, some more memory is saved as all texts and attribute values of the document are automatically indexed while parsing; the resulting indexes are also used for query processing. Last but not least, all texts in BASEX are internally stored in UTF8 byte arrays, which take less space than Java's UTF16 string representation for ASCII texts.

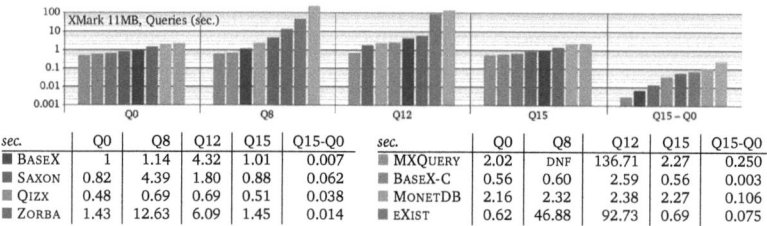

Figure 4.8: Processing four queries on an 11MB XMark instance.
DNF: did not finish within 5 min.

Next, four XMark queries were run on a smaller document instance. Figure 4.8 illustrates that a slow build process can be counterbalanced by fast query processing: while MONETDB needs longest for parsing the input, it shows very good performance for the join-based queries Q8 and Q12. BASEX is particularly good at optimizing and evaluating Q8, whereas it is outrun by other processors in Q12 and Q15. Due to its quick build time and join optimizations, QIXZ yielded good results for all four queries. Finally,

4.2. Querying

the last column of the table, which contains the arithmetic difference between *Q15* and *Q0*, shows a completely different picture: BASEX and ZORBA are very fast in processing simple *child* axes, after the document itself has been completely processed.

4.2.2.2 Database Processing

In this section, we will focus on the comparison of database engines. Accordingly, the tests will be limited to query processors that create a persistent representation of XML documents, and are backed by a client-/server architecture, namely BASEX, EXIST, and MONETDB. Just like in all prior tests, the processing time for an evaluating empty sequence was subtracted from the final results.

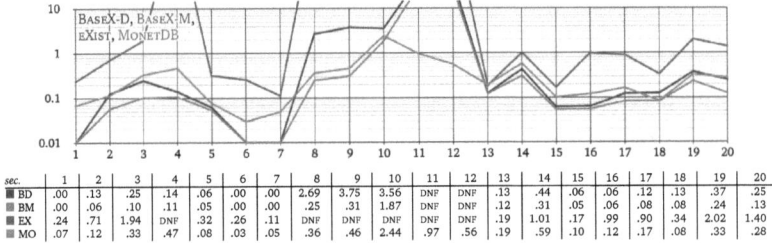

sec.	1	2	3	4	5	6	7	8	9	10	11	12	13	14	15	16	17	18	19	20
BD	.00	.13	.25	.14	.06	.00	.00	2.69	3.75	3.56	DNF	DNF	.13	.44	.06	.06	.12	.13	.37	.25
BM	.00	.06	.10	.11	.05	.00	.00	.25	.31	1.87	DNF	DNF	.12	.31	.05	.06	.08	.08	.24	.13
EX	.24	.71	1.94	DNF	.32	.26	.11	DNF	DNF	DNF	DNF	DNF	.19	1.01	.17	.99	.90	.34	2.02	1.40
MO	.07	.12	.33	.47	.08	.03	.05	.36	.46	2.44	.97	.56	.19	.59	.10	.12	.17	.08	.33	.28

Figure 4.9: Processing all XMark queries on a 111MB XMark instance.
DNF: did not finish within 5 min.

Figure 4.9 presents the time measurements for all 20 XMark queries, which are listed in full in Section 4.2.2.3. The 111MB document was chosen as input, as it was the largest instance that could be processed by all processors on the *Dual* test system with 2GB RAM (see Figure 4.3). MONETDB processes all database instances in main memory, while EXIST is disk-oriented. BASEX was tested both in its disk-based and main memory operating mode. The two modes, which will be abbreviated as BASEX-D and BASEX-M, use a similar internal representation of XML documents (see 2.5.3 for a reminder). As expected, the main memory mode of BASEX yielded better results for all queries, although the differences are sometimes marginal. This can be attributed to the caching behavior of the operating system, which enables quick access to all database blocks that have been touched at least once, and fit into main memory. The results will now be analyzed in detail:

- Query *Q1* contains a predicate with an equality comparison, which is rewritten by BASEX to an index access operator, followed by the inverted location path. As the index returns a single result, the whole query was evaluated in less than 5 ms, while MONETDB and EXIST needed 70 and 240 ms.

- Positional predicates are specified in *Q2* and *Q3*, and the resulting items are wrapped into new element nodes. BASEX-M offered the best performance, followed by BASEX-D and MONETDB.

- In Query *Q4*, nodes are filtered by their document order. Again, node comparisons are implemented most efficiently by BASEX, while EXIST failed to evaluate the query in the given time frame.

- A numerical comparison is defined in *Q5*, which was performed comparatively fast by all processors, especially by BASEX and MONETDB.

- Query *Q6* and *Q7* contain count() functions, which return the number of nodes found for specific location paths. Both queries were evaluated in constant time by BASEX: the traversal of the document is avoided, and the path summary is requested instead (see Figure 3.11). The results of EXIST and MONETDB indicate that a complete traversal of all descendants has been avoided here as well.

- Equi-joins on attribute values are specified in *Q8* and *Q9*. The attribute index is utilized in BASEX to avoid quadratic costs, as has been demonstrated in the query plans in Figure 3.12. This time, BASEX-D is about ten times slower than BASEX-M, as the index requests lead to numerous random disk accesses, which are evaluated much faster by the main memory index structures. MONETDB applies *loop lifting* for evaluating the nested loops [BGvK$^+$05] – which is an excellent alternative as long as enough main memory is available to the processor. EXIST was too slow to evaluate any of the five join queries (*Q8-Q12*)within in the maximum allowed time.

- Query *Q10* specifies another equi-join for comparing attribute values with the results of a distinct-values() function. A large output is generated, which contains numerous new elements. BASEX and MONETDB evaluated this query in a similar time: again, BASEX-M was slightly faster than MONETDB.

- Some more theta-joins are performed in *Q11* and *Q12*. This time, MONETDB was the only processor to return results in the specified time frame by *loop lifting* the join, whereas BASEX offers no optimizations for joins other than equality tests.

- All engines needed about the same time for evaluating Query *Q13*, which specifies a FLWOR expression with a simple location path and an element constructor. While

4.2. Querying

BaseX was slightly faster than its competitors, eXist managed to keep up with MonetDB.

- All engines showed competitive performance for *Q14*. This query is data intensive, as a contains() function is executed on numerous atomized text nodes.

- The Queries *Q15–Q17* contain simple location paths, which are composed of single *child* steps. The additional not() and empty() functions in *Q16*, which might be the reason for the decreased performance of the eXist engine, are removed by BaseX in the compilation phase.

- Query *Q18* contains a simple user-defined function, which is evaluated most efficiently by MonetDB. Performance could be further improved in BaseX by inlining the function (see Section 3.3.1.2 on the current state of the art).

- In Query *Q19*, most time is spent for sorting data. Again, BaseX-M performs best, closely followed by MonetDB and BaseX-D. BaseX uses an optimized *Quicksort* variant for sorting items [BM93].

- Finally, Query *Q20* groups the processed data into categories and returns the cardinalities. Both versions of BaseX managed to outrun their competitors.

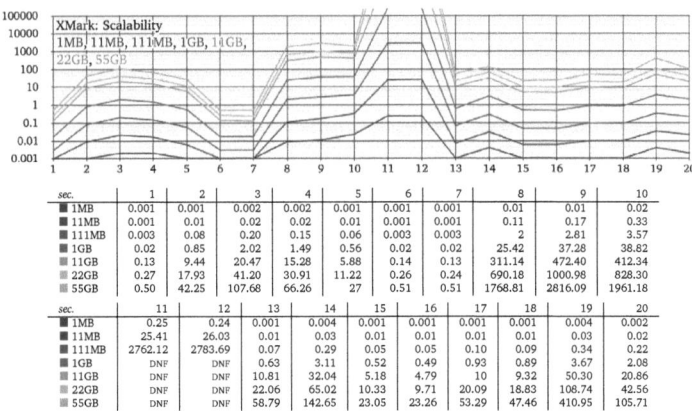

sec.	1	2	3	4	5	6	7	8	9	10
1MB	0.001	0.001	0.002	0.002	0.001	0.001	0.001	0.01	0.01	0.02
11MB	0.001	0.01	0.02	0.02	0.01	0.001	0.001	0.11	0.17	0.33
111MB	0.003	0.08	0.20	0.15	0.06	0.003	0.003	2	2.81	3.57
1GB	0.02	0.85	2.02	1.49	0.56	0.02	0.02	25.42	37.28	38.82
11GB	0.13	9.44	20.47	15.28	5.88	0.14	0.13	311.14	472.40	412.34
22GB	0.27	17.93	41.20	30.91	11.22	0.26	0.24	690.18	1000.98	828.30
55GB	0.50	42.25	107.68	66.26	27	0.51	0.51	1768.81	2816.09	1961.18

sec.	11	12	13	14	15	16	17	18	19	20
1MB	0.25	0.24	0.001	0.004	0.001	0.001	0.001	0.001	0.004	0.002
11MB	25.41	26.03	0.01	0.03	0.01	0.01	0.01	0.01	0.03	0.02
111MB	2762.12	2783.69	0.07	0.29	0.05	0.05	0.10	0.09	0.34	0.22
1GB	DNF	DNF	0.63	3.11	0.52	0.49	0.93	0.89	3.67	2.08
11GB	DNF	DNF	10.81	32.04	5.18	4.79	10	9.32	50.30	20.86
22GB	DNF	DNF	22.06	65.02	10.33	9.71	20.09	18.83	108.74	42.56
55GB	DNF	DNF	58.79	142.65	23.05	23.26	53.29	47.46	410.95	105.71

Figure 4.10: XMark Queries: Scalability of BaseX.
DNF: did not finish within 60 min.

To demonstrate that BaseX can easily process documents larger than 111MB, some other tests were performed on the *Xeon* test machine with 32GB RAM, the results of which are

4.2. Querying

shown in Figure 4.10. The XMark queries were run on seven XMark instances, ranging from 1MB to 55GB. The test conditions were slightly modified: The timeout was set to 60 minutes. The total runtime for testing a query was limited to 60 minutes as well, i.e., some queries were executed less than 15 times. Except for some queries on the 55GB instances that generate some additional overhead, such as Q8, Q9, or Q19, the system proved excellent scalability. Note that the good scalability is due to the large amount of RAM. BaseX is the only Open Source database architecture known to us, however, that allows it to perform XMark queries on instances larger than 11GB.

The query processor of BaseX has undergone several iterations before it has reached its present performance. While many optimizations have been too diversified to be briefly summarized, some of them have been presented in detail in Chapter 2 and 3, and will be highlighted again by analyzing the performance of different versions of BaseX in Figure 4.11:

sec.	1	2	3	4	5	6	7	8	9	10
4.0	.45	.56	.65	.33	.10	.61	1.33	DNF	DNF	DNF
5.0	.04	.23	.35	.21	.10	.42	.002	DNF	DNF	DNF
6.0	.001	.09	.20	.14	.06	.001	.002	DNF	DNF	DNF
6.3	.001	.09	.20	.13	.06	.001	.001	2.63	3.66	3.59
sec.	11	12	13	14	15	16	17	18	19	20
4.0	DNF	DNF	.15	.97	.12	.11	.19	.56	8.87	.44
5.0	DNF	DNF	.19	.97	.07	.06	.16	.25	.73	.31
6.0	DNF	DNF	.07	.44	.05	.04	.09	.09	.35	.21
6.3	DNF	DNF	.06	.40	.04	.04	.09	.09	.36	.22

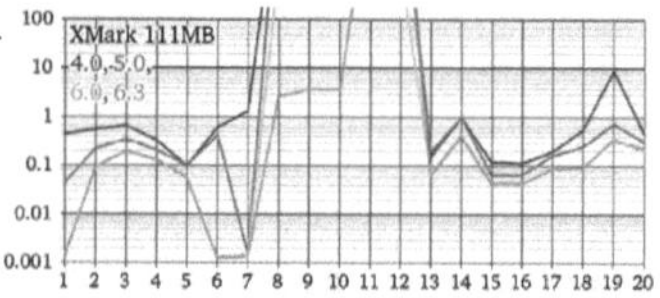

Figure 4.11: XMark Queries: Version history of BaseX.
DNF: did not finish within 5 min.

- The first optimizations were carried out on the storage backend: attributes (see 2.4.2.1) and numerical values (see 2.4.2.4) were inlined in the database table. The changes were done before Version 4.0, which was the first to fully support XQuery.

- Along with numerous other tweaks, iterative query evaluation was introduced with Version 5.0. As the diagram indicates, the performance was increased from 50% (Q15) up to 250% (Q2). The iterative traversal of location paths leads to a single scanning of the database table; before, it was scanned multiple times for each axis step. Next, the sort algorithm was improved to speed up the ORDER BY clause in Q19, and the statistics of the name indexes were taken advantage of to speed up the count() function of Q7.

- With Version 6.0, the index rewritings of location paths were generalized and extended to FLWOR expressions. As a result, Q1 is now evaluated via the attribute index. Q6 was optimized by accessing statistics from the path summary and pre-

4.2. Querying

evaluating the count() function on arbitrary paths with *child* steps. A general speedup for all location paths was achieved by reducing the number of temporary objects and reusing existing node instances, as described in 3.4.2.3.

- Advanced rewritings of FLWOR expressions were realized in the latest version (see Section 3.3.1.6). *Q8-Q10* and numerous other queries are now rewritten to take advantage of available content and full-text indexes.

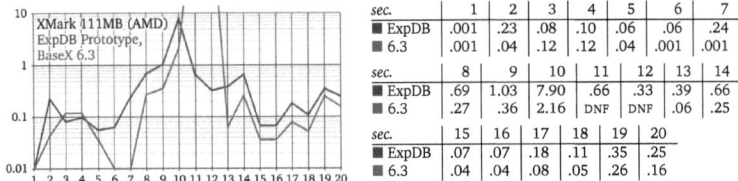

Figure 4.12: XMark Queries: Comparing BaseX 6.3 with results in [GHK⁺06]. DNF: did not finish within 5 min.

This section is concluded with another review of a prototype of BaseX, which has been compared with MonetDB in 2006 [GHK⁺06]. The XQuery expressions had been simulated with Java and XPath 1.0. At that time, we were confident that a future XQuery implementation would yield comparable results. Figure 4.12 demonstrates that the assumption was not only realistic, but was even exceeded. All tests were performed on the *AMD* architecture, which was also used for the published results. For most queries, the latest version of BaseX yields much better results than the former XPath implementation. Most time was saved for queries using the *child* step, as the original $pre/parent$ encoding was replaced by the $pre/dist/size$ representation. Next, the switch to the iterative processing model has been another important improvement, which is reflected by nearly all queries.

4.2.2.3 XMark Queries

In the following, all 20 XMark queries have been reprinted[2]. We have added two Queries *Q0* and *Q21*, which have additionally been used for testing.

Q0 Open document and return non-existing child comment nodes.

---

[2]Source: http://www.ins.cwi.nl/projects/xmark/Assets/xmlquery.txt

4.2. Querying

```
doc("xmark.xml")/comment()
```

Q1 Return the name of the person with ID 'person0'.
```
let $auction := doc("xmark.xml") return
for $b in $auction/site/people/person[@id = "person0"]
return $b/name/text()
```

Q2 Return the initial increases of all open auctions.
```
let $auction := doc("xmark.xml") return
for $b in $auction/site/open_auctions/open_auction
return <increase>{ $b/bidder[1]/increase/text() }</increase>
```

Q3 Return the IDs of all open auctions whose current increase is at least twice as high as the initial increase.
```
let $auction := doc("xmark.xml") return
for $b in $auction/site/open_auctions/open_auction
where zero-or-one($b/bidder[1]/increase/text()) * 2 <=
    $b/bidder[last()]/increase/text()
return <increase first="{$b/bidder[1]/increase/text()}"
                 last="{$b/bidder[last()]/increase/text()}"/>
```

Q4 List the reserves of those open auctions where a certain person issued a bid before another person.
```
let $auction := doc("xmark.xml") return
for $b in $auction/site/open_auctions/open_auction
where some $pr1 in $b/bidder/personref[@person = "person20"],
           $pr2 in $b/bidder/personref[@person = "person51"]
     satisfies $pr1 << $pr2
return <history>{$b/reserve/text()}</history>
```

Q5 How many sold items cost more than 40?
```
let $auction := doc("xmark.xml") return
count(for $i in $auction/site/closed_auctions/closed_auction
      where $i/price/text() >= 40
      return $i/price)
```

Q6 How many items are listed on all continents?
```
let $auction := doc("xmark.xml") return
for $b in $auction//site/regions
return count($b//item)
```

Q7 How many pieces of prose are in our database?
```
let $auction := doc("xmark.xml") return
for $p in $auction/site
return count($p//description) + count($p//annotation) + count($p//emailaddress)
```

Q8 List the names of persons and the number of items they bought.
```
let $auction := doc("xmark.xml") return
for $p in $auction/site/people/person
```

4.2. Querying

```
let $a := for $t in $auction/site/closed_auctions/closed_auction
            where $t/buyer/@person = $p/@id
            return $t
return <item person="{ $p/name/text() }">{ count($a) }</item>
```

Q9 List the names of persons and the names of the items they bought in Europe.

```
let $auction := doc("xmark.xml") return
let $ca := $auction/site/closed_auctions/closed_auction return
let $ei := $auction/site/regions/europe/item
for $p in $auction/site/people/person
let $a := for $t in $ca
            where $p/@id = $t/buyer/@person
            return let $n := for $t2 in $ei
                              where $t/itemref/@item = $t2/@id
                              return $t2
                   return <item>{ $n/name/text() }</item>
return <person name="{ $p/name/text() }">{ $a }</person>
```

Q10 List all persons according to their interest; use French markup in the result.

```
let $auction := doc("xmark.xml") return
for $i in distinct-values($auction/site/people/person/profile/interest/@category)
let $p := for $t in $auction/site/people/person
            where $t/profile/interest/@category = $i
            return
  <personne>
    <statistiques>
      <sexe>{$t/profile/gender/text()}</sexe>
      <age>{$t/profile/age/text()}</age>
      <education>{$t/profile/education/text()}</education>
      <revenu>{fn:data($t/profile/@income)}</revenu>
    </statistiques>
    <coordonnees>
      <nom>{$t/name/text()}</nom>
      <rue>{$t/address/street/text()}</rue>
      <ville>{$t/address/city/text()}</ville>
      <pays>{$t/address/country/text()}</pays>
      <reseau>
        <courrier>{$t/emailaddress/text()}</courrier>
        <pagePerso>{$t/homepage/text()}</pagePerso>
      </reseau>
    </coordonnees>
    <cartePaiement>{$t/creditcard/text()}</cartePaiement>
  </personne>
return <categorie>{ <id>{ $i }</id>, $p }</categorie>
```

Q11 For each person, list the number of items currently on sale whose price does not exceed 0.02% of the person's income.

```
let $auction := doc("xmark.xml") return
for $p in $auction/site/people/person
let $l := for $i in $auction/site/open_auctions/open_auction/initial
            where $p/profile/@income > 5000 * exactly-one($i/text())
            return $i
```

4.2. Querying

```
return <items name="{ $p/name/text() }">{ count($1) }</items>
```

Q12 For each richer-than-average person, list the number of items currently on sale whose price does not exceed 0.02% of the person's income.

```
let $auction := doc("xmark.xml") return
for $p in $auction/site/people/person
let $l := for $i in $auction/site/open_auctions/open_auction/initial
          where $p/profile/@income > 5000 * exactly-one($i/text())
          return $i
where $p/profile/@income > 50000
return <items person="{ $p/profile/@income }">{ count($1) }</items>
```

Q13 List the names of items registered in Australia along with their descriptions.

```
let $auction := doc("xmark.xml") return
for $i in $auction/site/regions/australia/item
return <item name="{ $i/name/text() }">{ $i/description }</item>
```

Q14 Return the names of all items whose description contains the word 'gold'.

```
let $auction := doc("xmark.xml") return
for $i in $auction/site//item
where contains(string(exactly-one($i/description)), "gold")
return $i/name/text()
```

Q15 Print the keywords in emphasis in annotations of closed auctions.

```
let $auction := doc("xmark.xml") return
for $a in $auction/site/closed_auctions/closed_auction/annotation/description/
  parlist/listitem/parlist/listitem/text/emph/keyword/text()
return <text>{ $a }</text>
```

Q16 Return the IDs of those auctions that have one or more keywords in emphasis.

```
let $auction := doc("xmark.xml") return
for $a in $auction/site/closed_auctions/closed_auction
where not(empty($a/annotation/description/parlist/listitem/parlist/listitem/text/
  emph/keyword/text()))
return <person id="{ $a/seller/@person }"/>
```

Q17 Which persons don't have a homepage?

```
let $auction := doc("xmark.xml") return
for $p in $auction/site/people/person
where empty($p/homepage/text())
return <person name="{ $p/name/text() }"/>
```

Q18 Convert the currency of the reserve of all open auctions to another currency.

```
declare namespace local = "http://www.foobar.org";
declare function local:convert($v as xs:decimal?) as xs:decimal? {
   2.20371 * $v (: convert Dfl to Euro :)
};
let $auction := doc("xmark.xml") return
for $i in $auction/site/open_auctions/open_auction
return local:convert(zero-or-one($i/reserve))
```

4.2. Querying

Q19 Give an alphabetically ordered list of all items along with their location.

```
let $auction := doc("xmark.xml") return
for $b in $auction/site/regions//item
let $k := $b/name/text()
order by zero-or-one($b/location) ascending empty greatest
return <item name="{ $k }">{ $b/location/text() }</item>
```

Q20 Group customers by their income and output the cardinality of each group.

```
let $auction := doc("xmark.xml") return
<result>
  <preferred>{
    count($auction/site/people/person/profile[@income >= 100000])
  }</preferred>
  <standard>{
    count($auction/site/people/person/
      profile[@income < 100000 and @income >= 30000])
  }</standard>
  <challenge>{
    count($auction/site/people/person/profile[@income < 30000])
  }</challenge>
  <na>{
    count(for $p in $auction/site/people/person
          where empty($p/profile/@income)
          return $p)
  }</na>
</result>
```

Q21 Return the category names of closed auctions in a certain price range.

```
let $auction := doc("xmark.xml") return
for $a in $auction/descendant::closed_auction[price >= 500 and price <= 1000]
for $i in $auction/descendant::item
for $c in $auction/descendant::category
where $a/itemref/@item = $i/@id and $c/@id = $i/incategory/@category
return $c/name
```

4.2.3 XQuery Full Text

BASEX was the first query processor to support the XQuery Full Text Recommendation (see 3.1.3), and, at the time of writing, it is still the only freely available implementation that works on large XML instances. This section presents some performance results on a complete XML dump of the English Wikipedia:

- Source: dumps.wikimedia.org/enwiki/latest/enwiki-latest-pages-articles.xml.bz2
- Accessed: 7 Jul 2010
- Document size: 25.4 GB
- XML nodes: 198.5 million
- Total database size: 45.4 GB (Full-text index: 20.0 GB)

4.2. Querying

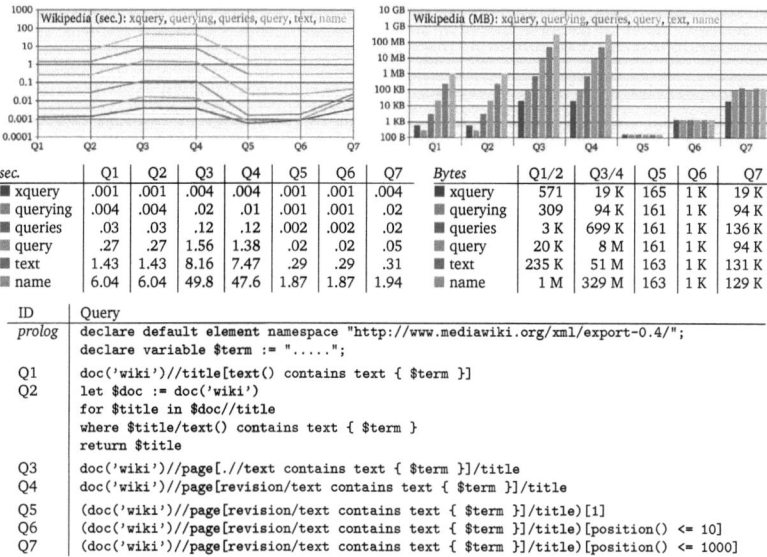

sec.	Q1	Q2	Q3	Q4	Q5	Q6	Q7	Bytes	Q1/2	Q3/4	Q5	Q6	Q7
■ xquery	.001	.001	.004	.004	.001	.001	.004	■ xquery	571	19 K	165	1 K	19 K
■ querying	.004	.004	.02	.01	.001	.001	.02	■ querying	309	94 K	161	1 K	94 K
■ queries	.03	.03	.12	.12	.002	.002	.02	■ queries	3 K	699 K	161	1 K	136 K
■ query	.27	.27	1.56	1.38	.02	.02	.05	■ query	20 K	8 M	161	1 K	94 K
■ text	1.43	1.43	8.16	7.47	.29	.29	.31	■ text	235 K	51 M	163	1 K	131 K
■ name	6.04	6.04	49.8	47.3	1.87	1.87	1.94	■ name	1 M	329 M	163	1 K	129 K

ID	Query
prolog	`declare default element namespace "http://www.mediawiki.org/xml/export-0.4/";` `declare variable $term := ".....";`
Q1	`doc('wiki')//title[text() contains text { $term }]`

Q2	`let $doc := doc('wiki')`
	`for $title in $doc//title`
	`where $title/text() contains text { $term }`
	`return $title`

Q3	`doc('wiki')//page[.//text contains text { $term }]/title`
Q4	`doc('wiki')//page[revision/text contains text { $term }]/title`
Q5	`(doc('wiki')//page[revision/text contains text { $term }]/title)[1]`
Q6	`(doc('wiki')//page[revision/text contains text { $term }]/title)[position() <= 10]`
Q7	`(doc('wiki')//page[revision/text contains text { $term }]/title)[position() <= 1000]`

Figure 4.13: English Wikipedia: Processing times and result sizes of seven full-text queries and six search terms

- Applied full-text index: Fuzzy Index
- Distinct full-text tokens: 42.9 million
- Index options: case/diacritics insensitive, no stemming/stopwords, default scoring

The client-/server-architecture of BASEX was used for all tests. The query results were written to a temporary file, and the mean of the total processing time of 5 runs, as returned by the following command call, was adopted for the figures:

```
java -cp basex-6.3.jar org.basex.BaseXClient -r5 -otmp -v query.xq
```

Figure 4.13 summarizes the results of the first test run, which demonstrates the scalability of the XQuery Full Text implementation. Each query is introduced with the *prolog*, shown in the table. Six different search terms were assigned to the $term variable, which served as input for the full-text expression of the queries *Q1-Q7* (totaling in 42 different queries):

- *Q1* and *Q2* return all titles that contain the specified search term. Both queries return the same results, as they are compiled and rewritten to the same internal,

4.2. Querying

index-based query plan. The FLWOR rewriting takes fractions of milliseconds; hence, it is not reflected in the result times.

- In *Q3* and *Q4*, the same text nodes are addressed by the full-text expression. Both queries return the titles of all pages that contain the specified term in the full-text. Due to the *descendant* step in the predicate, *Q3* is supposed to take slightly longer than *Q4*.

- *Q5-Q7* return the first 1, 10, and 1000 results of *Q4*.

The search terms were selected by their number of occurrences: the term *xquery* occurs in only 144 distinct text nodes, whereas the term *name* is placed 34th on the list of most frequent terms in the Wikipedia corpus, occurring in 2,65 million nodes and 10,54 million times in total[3]. This means that there are appr. 18,400 times more text nodes containing *name* than *xquery*. This difference is clearly reflected in the query results: while all queries for the term *xquery* are processed in less than 5 milliseconds, including the time for compiling the query and serializing the result, the output of 2,4 million titles, the articles of which contain the term *name*, takes about 50 seconds and produces 329 MiB of data. As can be seen in *Q5-Q7*, much time can be saved by limiting the number of results: the proportional difference for returning 1 or 1000 results is less than 10% of the the total processing time for queries with large result sets.

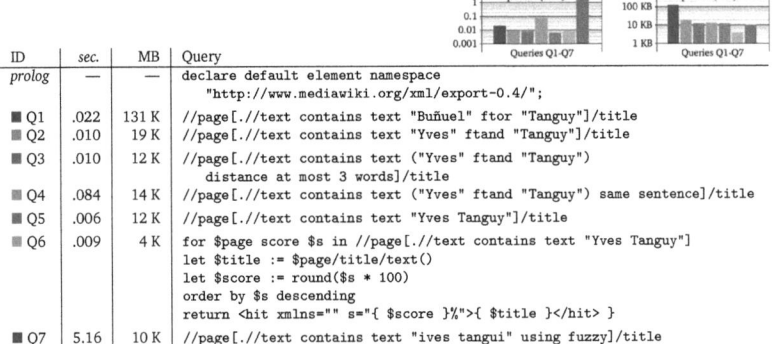

ID	sec.	MB	Query
prolog	—	—	declare default element namespace "http://www.mediawiki.org/xml/export-0.4/";
■ Q1	.022	131 K	//page[.//text contains text "Buñuel" ftor "Tanguy"]/title
■ Q2	.010	19 K	//page[.//text contains text "Yves" ftand "Tanguy"]/title
■ Q3	.010	12 K	//page[.//text contains text ("Yves" ftand "Tanguy") distance at most 3 words]/title
■ Q4	.084	14 K	//page[.//text contains text ("Yves" ftand "Tanguy") same sentence]/title
■ Q5	.006	12 K	//page[.//text contains text "Yves Tanguy"]/title
■ Q6	.009	4 K	for $page score $s in //page[.//text contains text "Yves Tanguy"] let $title := $page/title/text() let $score := round($s * 100) order by $s descending return <hit xmlns="" s="{ $score }%">{ $title }</hit> }
■ Q7	5.16	10 K	//page[.//text contains text "ives tangui" using fuzzy]/title

Figure 4.14: English Wikipedia: Processing times and result sizes of seven advanced full-text queries

---

[3]The BASEX command INFO INDEX FULLTEXT returns statistics on the full-text index structure.

4.2. Querying

Figure 4.14 shows the timings and result sizes of some more advanced XQuery Full Text expressions:

- *Q1* and *Q2* demonstrate the *logical connectives* `ftand` and `ftor`, which combine the results of two search tokens.

- *Q3* and *Q4* specify *positional filters*, namely a *distance* and a *scope selection*, to further restrict the results returned by the `ftand` operator.

- *Q5* performs a phrase search, which is comparable to a full-text query using `ftand`, a *distance* and an *ordered selection*.

- *Q6* calculates the score values of a location path with a full-text expression and a phrase as search token. All scores are sorted in a descending manner and embedded in new element fragments, along with the `title` elements of the original document.

- *Q7* demonstrates the BASEX specific *fuzzy match option*, which finds results that are equal or similar to the specified tokens.

As the performance results indicate, all expressions were rewritten to access the full-text index, and were evaluated in an iterative manner. Except for *Q4* and *Q7*, all queries are evaluated and serialized in a few milliseconds. For Query *Q4*, additional time is needed for computing the sentence positions of all tokens, as this information is not stored in the full-text index. The fuzzy option in *Q7* leads to a large number of intermediate results for the two single search terms, which are eventually combined to a small result set. – Last but not least, the first 12 results of *Q6* are printed in Table 4.4 and, for fun, compared with the results of a Google query to indicate that the default scoring yields good results:

BASEX, Q6 (first 12 of 90 results)	site:en.wikipedia.org "Yves Tanguy"
`<hit s="38%">Yves Tanguy</hit>`	1. Yves Tanguy
`<hit s="35%">File:Reply to Red.jpg</hit>`	2. File:Indefinite Divisibility.jpg
`<hit s="35%">File:Multiplication of the Arcs.jpg</hit>`	3. Tanguy
`<hit s="35%">File:Promontory Palace.jpg</hit>`	4. Kay Sage
`<hit s="34%">File:Mama, Papa is Wounded!.jpg</hit>`	5. File:Multiplication of the Arcs.jpg
`<hit s="33%">File:Indefinite Divisibility.jpg</hit>`	6. Surrealism
`<hit s="30%">Kay Sage</hit>`	7. Bodley Gallery
`<hit s="28%">Portal:Visual arts/Selected picture</hit>`	8. André Breton
`<hit s="26%">Tanguay</hit>`	9. File:Reply to Red.jpg
`<hit s="25%">Musick to Play in the Dark Vol. 1</hit>`	10. Tanguy (film)
`<hit s="24%">Biomorph</hit>`	11. File:Promontory Palace.jpg
`<hit s="24%">Surrealism</hit>`	12. Yves (given name)

Table 4.4: Wikipedia: Ranking results of Query *Q6*, compared with a Google query

4.3 Statistics

While many developers of scientific XML database prototypes and vendors of commercial systems claim that they can "large" or "huge" XML documents, it is difficult to find information on the factual limits of the presented architectures. It can be observed, instead, that most publications on XML processing limit performance tests to documents or collections of less than a Gigabyte, down to some Megabytes.

For this section, we first assembled the largest XML documents and collections that we could locate online and offline. While many of the documents are freely available, some of them have only been made available for testing purposes. Next, we approached the theoretical limits of our storage architecture, which have been elaborated in Section 2.4.1. We hope that the resulting survey, shown in Table 4.5, might be helpful for other XML developers as well. It offers the following information, specified in columns:

- *file size* represents the size of the original XML sources,
- *db size* is the size of the resulting database, excluding optional index structures,
- *#nodes* lists the number of unique XML nodes of a document,
- *#atr* reflects the maximum number of attribute nodes of a single element node,
- *#eln* and *#atn* represent the number of unique tag and attribute names,
- *#uri* indicates the number of distinct namespace URIs,
- *height* shows the tree height, and
- *#docs* contains the number of documents stored in the database.

The largest document we could get our hands – which was too large to be processed by BASEX – was the complete, zipped dump of the Wikipedia Encyclopedia[4], occupying more than 3 TiB in a single file. References to all documents and collections (or the homepages of its suppliers) that have been used for creating the survey are listed in Table 4.6.

---

[4]XML dump of the Wikipedia, containing all pages with complete edit history:
http://download.wikimedia.org/enwiki/latest/pages-meta-history.xml.7z

4.3. Statistics

Instances	file size	db size	#nodes	#atr	#eln	#atn	#uri	height	#docs
RuWikiHist	421 GiB	416 GiB	324,848,508	3	21	6	2	6	1
ZhWikiHist	126 GiB	120 GiB	179,199,662	3	21	6	2	6	1
EnWiktionary	79 GiB	75 GiB	134,380,393	3	21	6	2	6	1
XMark	55 GiB	64 GiB	1,615,071,348	2	74	9	0	13	1
EnWikiMeta	54 GiB	52 GiB	401,456,348	3	21	6	2	6	1
MedLine	38 GiB	36 GiB	1,623,764,254	2	84	6	0	9	379
iProClass	36 GiB	37 GiB	1,631,218,984	3	245	4	2	9	1
Inex209	31 GiB	34 GiB	1,336,110,639	15	28,034	451	1	37	2,666,500
CoPhIR	29 GiB	31 GiB	1,104,623,376	10	42	42	0	8	10,000,000
EnWikipedia	26 GiB	25 GiB	198,546,747	3	24	21	2	6	1
XMark	22 GiB	26 GiB	645,997,965	2	74	9	0	13	1
InterPro	14 GiB	19 GiB	860,304,235	5	7	15	0	4	1
Genome1	13 GiB	13 GiB	432,628,105	12	26	101	2	6	1
NewYorkTimes	12 GiB	13 GiB	280,407,005	5	41	33	0	6	1,855,659
TrEMBL	11 GiB	14 GiB	589,650,535	8	47	30	2	7	1
XMark	11 GiB	13 GiB	323,083,409	2	74	9	0	13	1
IntAct	7973 MiB	6717 MiB	297,478,392	7	64	22	2	14	25,624
Freebase	7366 MiB	10 GiB	443,627,994	8	61	283	1	93	1
SDMX	6356 MiB	8028 MiB	395,871,872	2	22	6	3	7	1
OpenStreetMap	5312 MiB	5171 MiB	6,910,669	3	19	5	2	6	1
SwissProt	4604 MiB	5422 MiB	241,274,406	8	70	39	2	7	1
EurLex	4815 MiB	5532 MiB	167,328,039	23	186	46	1	12	1
Wikicorpus	4492 MiB	4432 MiB	157,948,561	12	1,257	2,687	2	50	659,338
EnWikiRDF	3679 MiB	3537 MiB	98,433,194	1	11	2	11	4	1
CoPhIR	2695 MiB	2882 MiB	101,638,857	10	42	42	0	8	1,000,000
MeSH	2091 MiB	2410 MiB	104,845,819	3	6	5	2	5	1
FreeDB	1723 MiB	2462 MiB	102,901,519	2	7	3	0	4	1
XMark	1134 MiB	1303 MiB	32,298,989	2	74	9	0	13	1
DeepFS	810 MiB	850 MiB	44,821,506	4	3	6	0	24	1
LibraryUKN	760 MiB	918 MiB	46,401,941	3	23	3	0	5	1
Twitter	736 MiB	767 MiB	15,309,015	0	8	0	0	3	1,177,495
Organizations	733 MiB	724 MiB	33,112,392	3	38	9	0	7	1,019,132
DBLP	694 MiB	944 MiB	36,878,181	4	35	6	0	7	1
Feeds	692 MiB	604 MiB	5,933,713	0	8	0	0	3	444,014
MedLineSupp	477 MiB	407 MiB	21,602,141	5	55	7	0	9	1
AirBase	449 MiB	273 MiB	14,512,851	1	111	5	0	11	38
MedLineDesc	260 MiB	195 MiB	10,401,847	5	66	8	0	9	1
ZDNet	130 MiB	133 MiB	3,060,186	21	40	90	0	13	95,663
JMNedict	124 MiB	171 MiB	8,592,666	0	10	0	0	5	1
XMark	111 MiB	130 MiB	3,221,926	2	74	9	0	13	1
Freshmeat	105 MiB	86 MiB	3,832,028	1	58	1	0	6	1
DeepFS	83 MiB	93 MiB	4,842,638	4	3	6	0	21	1
Treebank	82 MiB	92 MiB	3,829,513	1	250	1	0	37	1
DBLP2	80 MiB	102 MiB	4,044,649	4	35	6	0	6	170,843
DDI	76 MiB	39 MiB	2,070,157	7	104	16	21	11	3
Alfred	75 MiB	68 MiB	3,784,285	0	60	0	0	6	1
University	56 MiB	66 MiB	3,468,606	1	28	4	0	5	6
MediaUKN	38 MiB	45 MiB	1,619,443	3	21	3	0	5	1
HCIBIB2	32 MiB	33 MiB	617,023	1	39	1	0	4	26,390
Nasa	24 MiB	25 MiB	845,805	2	61	8	1	9	1
MovieDB	16 MiB	19 MiB	868,980	6	7	8	0	4	1
KanjiDic2	13 MiB	18 MiB	917,833	3	27	10	0	6	1
XMark	11 MiB	13 MiB	324,274	2	74	9	0	13	1
Shakespeare	7711 KiB	9854 KiB	327,170	0	59	0	0	9	1
TreeOfLife	5425 KiB	7106 KiB	363,560	7	4	7	0	243	1
Thesaurus	4288 KiB	4088 KiB	201,798	7	33	9	0	7	1
MusicXML	3155 KiB	2942 KiB	171,400	8	179	56	0	8	17
BibDBPub	2292 KiB	2359 KiB	80,178	1	54	1	0	4	3,465
Factbook	1743 KiB	1560 KiB	77,315	16	23	32	0	6	1
XMark	1134 KiB	1334 KiB	33,056	2	74	9	0	13	1

Table 4.5: Statistics on selected XML documents and collections

4.3. Statistics

Instances	Source
AirBase	air-climate.eionet.europa.eu/databases/airbase/airbasexml
Alfred	alfred.med.yale.edu/alfred/alfredWithDescription.zip
BibDBPub	inex.is.informatik.uni-duisburg.de/2005
CoPhIR	cophir.isti.cnr.it
DBLP	dblp.uni-trier.de/xml
DBLP2	inex.is.informatik.uni-duisburg.de/2005
DDI	tools.ddialliance.org
EnWikiMeta	dumps.wikimedia.org/enwiki/latest/enwiki-latest-pages-meta-current.xml.bz2
EnWikipedia	dumps.wikimedia.org/enwiki/latest/enwiki-latest-pages-articles.xml.bz2
EnWikiRDF	www.xml-benchmark.org: generated with xmlgen
EnWiktionary	wikimedia.org/enwiktionary/latest (pages-meta-history.xml.7z)
EurLex	www.epsiplatform.eu
Factbook	www.cs.washington.edu/research/xmldatasets/www/repository.html
Freebase	download.freebase.com/wex
FreeDB	www.xmldatabases.org/radio/xmlDatabases/projects/FreeDBtoXML
Freshmeat	freshmeat.net/articles/freshmeat-xml-rpc-api-available
Genome1	ftp.ncbi.nih.gov/snp/organisms/human_9606/XML/ds_ch1.xml.gz
HCIBIB2	inex.is.informatik.uni-duisburg.de/2005
Inex2009	www.mpi-inf.mpg.de/departments/d5/software/inex
IntAct	ftp.ebi.ac.uk/pub/databases/intact/current/index.html
InterPro	ftp.bio.net/biomirror/interpro/match_complete.xml.gz
iProClass	ftp.pir.georgetown.edu/pir_databases/iproclass/iproclass.xml.gz
JMnEdict	ftp.monash.edu.au/pub/nihongo/enamdict_doc.html
KanjiDic2	www.csse.monash.edu.au/jwb/kanjidic2
MedLine	www.nlm.nih.gov/bsd
MeSH	www.nlm.nih.gov/mesh/xmlmesh.html
MovieDB	InfoVis 2007 Contest: IMDB Data
MusicXML	www.recordare.com/xml/samples.html
Nasa	www.cs.washington.edu/research/xmldatasets/www/repository.html
NewYorkTimes	www.nytimes.com/ref/membercenter/nytarchive.html
OpenStreetMap	dump.wiki.openstreetmap.org/osmwiki-latest-files.tar.gz
Organizations	www.data.gov/raw/1358
RuWikiHist	dumps.wikimedia.org/ruwiki/latest/ruwiki-latest-pages-meta-history.xml.7z
SDMX	www.metadatatechnology.com
Shakespeare	www.cafeconleche.org/examples/shakespeare
SwissProt	ftp.uniprot.org/pub/databases/uniprot/current_release/knowledgebase
Thesaurus	www.drze.de/BELIT/thesaurus
Treebank	www.cs.washington.edu/research/xmldatasets
TreeOfLife	tolweb.org/data/tolskeletaldump.xml
TrEMBL	ftp.uniprot.org/pub/databases/uniprot/current_release/knowledgebase
Wikicorpus	www-connex.lip6.fr/ denoyer/wikipediaXML
XMark	www.xml-benchmark.org: generated with xmlgen
ZDNET	inex.is.informatik.uni-duisburg.de/2005
ZhWikiHist	dumps.wikimedia.org/zhwiki/latest/zhwiki-latest-pages-meta-history.xml.7z
LibraryUKN	generated from university library data
MediaUKN	generated from university library data
DeepFS	generated from filesystem structure
University	generated from students test data
Feeds	compiled from news feeds
Twitter	compiled from Twitter feeds

Table 4.6: References to document sources (last accessed: 1 Oct 2010)

5 Conclusion

XML is here to stay – and so are techniques for storing and querying XML. In this thesis, we hope to have shown that a database architecture needs to rely on both theoretical and practical aspects to cover the demands of real-life applications and workloads. While this may sound hackneyed, we have frequently come across counter examples, which either focused on theoretical, albeit artificial scenarios, or which lacked a solid theoretical background to be extensible enough for advanced use cases.

As a final conclusion, we have summarized the major contributions of this thesis:

- **Section 2.4**: We have presented *Pre/Dist/Size* as a powerful encoding for mapping XML data to flat tables: the $size$ property facilitates quick access to descendants and following siblings of an XML node, and the $dist$ property serves as direct, *update-invariant* parent reference.

- **Section 2.4.1.2**: Using our architecture, we have collected statistical data of a wide range of *large-scale*, real-life XML documents and collections. While the resulting information was primarily evaluated to find a good tradeoff between a minimum database size and maximum input document size, we also believe it represents one of the most comprehensive surveys on large XML instances that has been published so far.

- **Section 2.4.2**: The proposed encoding is represented in a single *compactified*, fixed-size tuple of 16 bytes. Static and redundant information were dropped, and numerical document contents were *inlined* in the tuple. Next, attribute nodes were *inlined* as well, i.e., stored in the same way as other XML nodes. This way, both memory is saved and queries are accelerated.

- **Section 2.6**: In contrast to other data structures, our storage can be easily extended by various structural and content-based *index structures*, which provide a base for accelerating many queries by orders of magnitudes.

- **Section 3.3.1**: In the *Querying* chapter, a thorough insight is given how classical and XML-specific *optimizations* can be applied to arbitrary XQuery processors.

- **Section 3.3.2**: We were the first, to the best of our knowledge, to describe how location paths with equality tests or full-text expressions as predicates can be rewritten for accessing *index structures* of an underlying database. This optimization, which is comparatively straightforward in relational databases, requires that many preconditions are met in the context of XPath/XQuery.

- **Section 3.4.1**: We have shown how an adaptive evaluation approach can be realized to benefit from both the *iterative* and *atomic* processing paradigm.

- **Section 3.4.2**: Based on our *Pre/Dist/Size* encoding, the *traversal* of location paths and all XPath axes was illustrated.

- **Section 3.5**: A detailed *summary* describes what optimizations exist for the most important XQuery expressions. We hope that other implementors of XQuery might benefit from this summary, too.

- Finally, **Chapter 4** demonstrates that the chosen architecture yields excellent performance results, both regarding efficiency and scalability.

In short, we believe that the proposed storage and query architecture represents a powerful yet light-weight framework for both processing very large XML instances and evaluating queries with impressive performance. The Open Source database system BASEX represents an elaborate proof of concept for the ideas discussed in this work.

Bibliography

[ABC+99] Vidur Apparao, Steve Byrne, Mike Champion, Scott Isaacs, Ian Jacobs, Arnaud Le Hors, Gavin Nicol, Jonathan Robie, Robert Sutor, Chris Wilson, and Lauren Wood. Document Object Model Level 1. http://www.w3.org/DOM, October 1999.

[ABF+09] Cezar Andrei, Matthias Brantner, Daniela Florescu, David Graf, Donald Kossmann, and Markos Zacharioudakis. Extending XQuery with Collections, Indexes, and Integrity Constraints, Working Draft, 2009. http://www.flworfound.org/pubs/xqddf.pdf, 2009.

[Abi97] Serge Abiteboul. Querying Semi-Structured Data. In *ICDT*, volume 1186 of *Lecture Notes in Computer Science*, pages 1–18. Springer, 1997.

[AMS92] Jun-Ichi Aoe, Katsushi Morimoto, and Takashi Sato. An Efficient Implementation of Trie Structures. *Softw., Pract. Exper.*, 22(9):695–721, 1992.

[AOV+99] Malcolm P. Atkinson, Maria E. Orlowska, Patrick Valduriez, Stanley B. Zdonik, and Michael L. Brodie, editors. *VLDB'99, Proceedings of 25th International Conference on Very Large Data Bases, September 7-10, 1999, Edinburgh, Scotland, UK*. Morgan Kaufmann, 1999.

[AQM+97] Serge Abiteboul, Dallan Quass, Jason McHugh, Jennifer Widom, and Janet L. Wiener. The Lorel Query Language for Semistructured Data. *Int. J. on Digital Libraries*, 1(1):68–88, 1997.

[AS08] Ramez Alkhatib and Marc H. Scholl. CXQU: A compact XML storage for efficient query and update processing. In *ICDIM*, pages 605–612. IEEE, 2008.

[AS09] Ramez Alkhatib and Marc H. Scholl. Compacting XML Structures Using a Dynamic Labeling Scheme. In *BNCOD*, volume 5588 of *Lecture Notes in Computer Science*, pages 158–170. Springer, 2009.

Bibliography

[AYBB+09] Sihem Amer-Yahia, Chavdar Botev, Stephen Buxton, Pat Case, Jochen Doerre, et al. XQuery and XPath Full Text 1.0. W3C Candidate Recommendation. http://www.w3.org/TR/xpath-full-text-10, July 2009.

[BBB00] Ron Bourret, Christof Bornhövd, and Alejandro P. Buchmann. A Generic Load/Extract Utility for Data Transfer between XML Documents and Relational Databases. In *WECWIS*, pages 134–143, 2000.

[BCF+07] Scott Boag, Don Chamberlin, Mary F. Fernández, Daniela Florescu, Jonathan Robie, and Jérôme Siméon. XQuery 1.0: An XML Query Language. W3C Recommendation. http://www.w3.org/TR/xquery, January 2007.

[BGvK+05] Peter A. Boncz, Torsten Grust, Maurice van Keulen, Stefan Manegold, Jan Rittinger, and Jens Teubner. Pathfinder: XQuery - The Relational Way. In *VLDB*, pages 1322–1325. ACM, 2005.

[Bib99] Die Deutsche Bibliothek. *MAB2: Maschinelles Austauschformat für Bibliotheken*. Die Deutsche Bibliothek, Leipzig/Frankfurt am Main, second edition, 1999.

[BIRP02] Philip A. Bernstein, Yannis E. Ioannidis, Raghu Ramakrishnan, and Dimitris Papadias, editors. *VLDB 2002, Proceedings of 28th International Conference on Very Large Data Bases, August 20-23, 2002, Hong Kong, China*. Morgan Kaufmann, 2002.

[BK89] Elisa Bertino and Won Kim. Indexing Techniques for Queries on Nested Objects. *IEEE Trans. Knowl. Data Eng.*, 1(2):196–214, 1989.

[BKT+07] Scott Boag, Michael Kay, Joanne Tong, Norman Walsh, and Henry Zongaro. XSLT 2.0 and XQuery 1.0 Serialization. http://www.w3.org/TR/xslt-xquery-serialization, January 2007.

[BM72] Rudolf Bayer and Edward M. McCreight. Organization and Maintenance of Large Ordered Indices. *Acta Inf.*, 1:173–189, 1972.

[BM93] Jon Louis Bentley and M. Douglas McIlroy. Engineering a Sort Function. *Softw., Pract. Exper.*, 23(11):1249–1265, 1993.

[BMR05] Peter A. Boncz, Stefan Manegold, and Jan Rittinger. Updating the Pre/Post Plane in MonetDB/XQuery. In *XIME-P*, 2005.

Bibliography

[Boa05] Scott Boag. Building a Tokenizer for XPath or XQuery. http://www.w3.org/TR/xquery-xpath-parsing, April 2005.

[Bot04] Per Bothner. Compiling XQuery to Java Bytecodes. In *XIME-P*, pages 31–36, 2004.

[BPSM+08] Tim Bray, Jean Paoli, C. M. Sperberg-McQueen, Eve Maler, et al. Extensible Markup Language (XML) 1.0 (Fifth Edition). http://www.w3.org/TR/xml, November 2008.

[BSAY04] Chavdar Botev, Jayavel Shanmugasundaram, and Sihem Amer-Yahia. A TeXQuery-Based XML Full-Text Search Engine. In Weikum et al. [WKD04], pages 943–944.

[Bun97] Peter Buneman. Semistructured Data. In *PODS*, pages 117–121. ACM Press, 1997.

[CB74] Donald D. Chamberlin and Raymond F. Boyce. SEQUEL: A Structured English Query Language. In *SIGMOD Workshop, Vol. 1*, pages 249–264. ACM, 1974.

[CD99] James Clark and Steven J. DeRose. XML Path Language (XPath) Version 1.0. W3C Recommendation. http://www.w3.org/TR/xpath, November 1999.

[CD07] James Clark and Steven J. DeRose. XML Path Language (XPath) Version 2.0. W3C Recommendation. http://www.w3.org/TR/xpath20, January 2007.

[CDF+09] Don Chamberlin, Michael Dyck, Daniela Florescu, Jim Melton, Jonathan Robie, and Jérôme Siméon. XQuery Update Facility. http://www.w3.org/TR/xqupdate, June 2009.

[CEF+08] Don Chamberlin, Daniel Engovatov, Dana Florescu, Giorgio Ghelli, Jim Melton, Jérôme Siméon, and John Snelson. XQuery Scripting Extension 1.0. http://www.w3.org/TR/xquery-sx-10, April 2008.

[CKM02] Edith Cohen, Haim Kaplan, and Tova Milo. Labeling Dynamic XML Trees. In *PODS*, pages 271–281. ACM, 2002.

[Cla99] James Clark. XSL Transformations (XSLT) Version 1.0. http://www.w3.org/TR/xslt, November 1999.

Bibliography

[CMS02] Chin-Wan Chung, Jun-Ki Min, and Kyuseok Shim. APEX: an adaptive path index for XML data. In Franklin et al. [FMA02], pages 121–132.

[CMV05] Barbara Catania, Anna Maddalena, and Athena Vakali. XML Document Indexes: A Classification. *IEEE Internet Computing*, 9(5):64–71, 2005.

[Cow08] John Cowan. TagSoup. http://ccil.org/~cowan/XML/tagsoup, 2008.

[CRF00] Donald D. Chamberlin, Jonathan Robie, and Daniela Florescu. Quilt: An XML Query Language for Heterogeneous Data Sources. In *WebDB (Selected Papers)*, volume 1997 of *Lecture Notes in Computer Science*, pages 1–25. Springer, 2000.

[Cro06] Douglas Crockford. JSON: The Fat-Free Alternative to XML. In *XML*, 2006.

[Dam64] Fred Damerau. A technique for computer detection and correction of spelling errors. *Commun. ACM*, 7(3):171–176, 1964.

[DFF+98] Alin Deutsch, Mary F. Fernández, Daniela Florescu, Alon Y. Levy, and Dan Suciu. XML-QL. In *QL*, 1998.

[DFF+99] Alin Deutsch, Mary F. Fernández, Daniela Florescu, Alon Y. Levy, and Dan Suciu. A Query Language for XML. *Computer Networks*, 31(11-16):1155–1169, 1999.

[DFF+07] Denise Draper, Peter Fankhauser, Mary F. Fernández, Ashok Malhotra, Kristoffer Rose, Michael Rys, Jérôme Siméon, and Philip Wadler. XQuery 1.0 and XPath 2.0 Formal Semantics. http://www.w3.org/TR/xquery-semantics, January 2007.

[DFS99] Alin Deutsch, Mary F. Fernández, and Dan Suciu. Storing Semistructured Data with STORED. In *SIGMOD Conference*, pages 431–442. ACM Press, 1999.

[Die82] Paul F. Dietz. Maintaining Order in a Linked List. In *STOC*, pages 122–127. ACM, 1982.

[ECM06] ECMA. *ECMA-376: Office Open XML File Formats*. ECMA (European Association for Standardizing Information and Communication Systems), 2006.

[EH00] Richard Edwards and Sian Hope. Persistent DOM: An Architecture for XML Repositories in Relational Databases. In *IDEAL*, volume 1983 of *Lecture Notes in Computer Science*, pages 416–421. Springer, 2000.

Bibliography

[FG89] Johann Christoph Freytag and Nathan Goodman. On the Translation of Relational Queries into Iterative Programs. *ACM Trans. Database Syst.*, 14(1):1–27, 1989.

[FHK+02] Thorsten Fiebig, Sven Helmer, Carl-Christian Kanne, Guido Moerkotte, Julia Neumann, Robert Schiele, and Till Westmann. Anatomy of a native XML base management system. *VLDB J.*, 11(4):292–314, 2002.

[FHK+03] Daniela Florescu, Chris Hillery, Donald Kossmann, Paul Lucas, Fabio Riccardi, Till Westmann, Michael J. Carey, Arvind Sundararajan, and Geetika Agrawal. The BEA/XQRL Streaming XQuery Processor. In Freytag et al. [FLA+03], pages 997–1008.

[FHK+04] Daniela Florescu, Chris Hillery, Donald Kossmann, Paul Lucas, Fabio Riccardi, Till Westmann, Michael J. Carey, and Arvind Sundararajan. The BEA streaming XQuery processor. *VLDB J.*, 13(3):294–315, 2004.

[FK99] Daniela Florescu and Donald Kossmann. Storing and Querying XML Data using an RDMBS. *IEEE Data Eng. Bull.*, 22(3):27–34, 1999.

[FLA+03] Johann Christoph Freytag, Peter C. Lockemann, Serge Abiteboul, Michael J. Carey, Patricia G. Selinger, and Andreas Heuer, editors. *VLDB 2003, Proceedings of 29th International Conference on Very Large Data Bases, September 9-12, 2003, Berlin, Germany*. Morgan Kaufmann, 2003.

[FMA02] Michael J. Franklin, Bongki Moon, and Anastassia Ailamaki, editors. *Proceedings of the 2002 ACM SIGMOD International Conference on Management of Data, Madison, Wisconsin, June 3-6, 2002*. ACM, 2002.

[FMM+07] Mary Fernández, Ashok Malhotra, Jonathan Marsh, Marton Nagy, and Norman Walsh. XQuery 1.0 and XPath 2.0 Data Model. http://www.w3.org/TR/xpath-datamodel, January 2007.

[Fre60] Edward Fredkin. Trie Memory. *j-CACM*, 3(9):490–499, 1960.

[FRSV05] Achille Fokoue, Kristoffer Høgsbro Rose, Jérôme Siméon, and Lionel Villard. Compiling XSLT 2.0 into XQuery 1.0. In *WWW*, pages 682–691. ACM, 2005.

[Gat09] Sebastian Gath. Verarbeitung und Visualisierung von XML-Full-Text Daten. Master's thesis, University of Konstanz, Germany, May 2009.

Bibliography

[GC07] Gang Gou and Rada Chirkova. Efficiently Querying Large XML Data Repositories: A Survey. *IEEE Trans. Knowl. Data Eng.*, 19(10):1381–1403, 2007.

[GCCM98] Roy Goldman, Sudarshan Chawathe, Arturo Crespo, and Jason McHugh. A Standard Textual Interchange Format for the Object Exchange Model (OEM). Technical Report CS-TN-98-64, Stanford University, Stanford, CA, 1998.

[GGHS09a] Christian Grün, Sebastian Gath, Alexander Holupirek, and Marc H. Scholl. INEX Efficiency Track meets XQuery Full Text in BaseX. In *Pre-Proceedings of the 8th INEX Workshop*, pages 192–197, 2009.

[GGHS09b] Christian Grün, Sebastian Gath, Alexander Holupirek, and Marc H. Scholl. XQuery Full Text Implementation in BaseX. In *XSym*, volume 5679 of *Lecture Notes in Computer Science*, pages 114–128. Springer, 2009.

[GGJ+05] Christian Grün, Jens Gerken, Hans-Christian Jetter, Werner A. König, and Harald Reiterer. MedioVis – A User-Centred Library Metadata Browser. In *ECDL*, volume 3652 of *Lecture Notes in Computer Science*, pages 174–185. Springer, 2005.

[GHK+06] Christian Grün, Alexander Holupirek, Marc Kramis, Marc H. Scholl, and Marcel Waldvogel. Pushing XPath Accelerator to its Limits. In *ExpDB*. ACM, 2006.

[GHS07] Christian Grün, Alexander Holupirek, and Marc H. Scholl. Visually Exploring and Querying XML with BaseX. In *BTW*, volume 103 of *LNI*, pages 629–632. GI, 2007.

[GK02] Maxim Grinev and Sergei D. Kuznetsov. Towards an Exhaustive Set of Rewriting Rules for XQuery Optimization: BizQuery Experience. In *ADBIS*, volume 2435 of *Lecture Notes in Computer Science*, pages 340–345. Springer, 2002.

[GL04] Maxim Grinev and Dmitry Lizorkin. XQuery Function Inlining for Optimizing XQuery Queries. In *ADBIS*, volume 3255 of *Lecture Notes in Computer Science*. Springer, 2004.

[GMR+07] Torsten Grust, Manuel Mayr, Jan Rittinger, Sherif Sakr, and Jens Teubner. A SQL: 1999 Code Generator for the Pathfinder XQuery Compiler. In *SIGMOD Conference*, pages 1162–1164. ACM, 2007.

Bibliography

[Gra93]   Goetz Graefe. Query Evaluation Techniques for Large Databases. *ACM Comput. Surv.*, 25(2):73–170, 1993.

[Gru02]   Torsten Grust. Accelerating XPath location steps. In Franklin et al. [FMA02], pages 109–120.

[Grü06]   Christian Grün. Pushing XML Main Memory Databases to their Limits. In *Grundlagen von Datenbanken*, pages 60–64. Institute of Computer Science, Martin-Luther-University, 2006.

[Grü10]   Christian Grün. BaseX – The XML Database for Processing, Querying and Visualizing large XML data. http://basex.org, October 2010.

[GSBS03] Lin Guo, Feng Shao, Chavdar Botev, and Jayavel Shanmugasundaram. XRANK: Ranked Keyword Search over XML Documents. In *SIGMOD Conference*, pages 16–27. ACM, 2003.

[GT04]   Torsten Grust and Jens Teubner. Relational Algebra: Mother Tongue – XQuery: Fluent. In *TDM*, CTIT Workshop Proceedings Series, pages 9–16. Centre for Telematics and Information Technology (CTIT), University of Twente, Enschede, The Netherlands, 2004.

[GVK04]   Torsten Grust, Roel Vercammen, and Maurice Van Keulen. Supporting Positional Predicates in Efficient XPath Axis Evaluation for DOM Data Structures. Technical Report TR 2004-05, University of Antwerp, 2004.

[GvKT03] Torsten Grust, Maurice van Keulen, and Jens Teubner. Staircase Join: Teach a Relational DBMS to Watch its (Axis) Steps. In Freytag et al. [FLA$^+$03], pages 524–525.

[GW89]   Goetz Graefe and Karen Ward. Dynamic Query Evaluation Plans. In *SIGMOD Conference*, pages 358–366. ACM Press, 1989.

[GW97]   Roy Goldman and Jennifer Widom. DataGuides: Enabling Query Formulation and Optimization in Semistructured Databases. In *VLDB*, pages 436–445. Morgan Kaufmann, 1997.

[Hau09]   Jörg Hauser. Entwicklung effizienter Treemap-Visualisierungen im XML-Kontext. Bachelor's Thesis, University of Konstanz, Germany, November 2009.

Bibliography

[HGS09] Alexander Holupirek, Christian Grün, and Marc H. Scholl. BaseX & DeepFS – Joint Storage for Filesystem and Database. In *EDBT*, volume 360 of *ACM International Conference Proceeding Series*, pages 1108–1111. ACM, 2009.

[HHMW07] Theo Härder, Michael Peter Haustein, Christian Mathis, and Markus Wagner. Node labeling schemes for dynamic XML documents reconsidered. *Data Knowl. Eng.*, 60(1):126–149, 2007.

[HM99] Gerald Huck and Ingo Macherius. GMD-IPSI XQL Engine. http://xml.darmstadt.gmd.de/xql, 1999.

[HMV05] Jan Hidders, Philippe Michiels, and Roel Vercammen. Optimizing Sorting and Duplicate Elimination in XQuery Path Expressions. *Bulletin of the EATCS*, 86:199–223, 2005.

[Ioa96] Yannis E. Ioannidis. Query Optimization. *ACM Comput. Surv.*, 28(1):121–123, 1996.

[JAKC+02] H. V. Jagadish, Shurug Al-Khalifa, Adriane Chapman, Laks V. S. Lakshmanan, Andrew Nierman, Stelios Paparizos, Jignesh M. Patel, Divesh Srivastava, Nuwee Wiwatwattana, Yuqing Wu, and Cong Yu. TIMBER: A native XML database. *VLDB J.*, 11(4):274–291, 2002.

[Joh84] Thomas Johnsson. Efficient compilation of lazy evaluation. In *SIGPLAN Symposium on Compiler Construction*, pages 58–69. ACM, 1984.

[Kay04] Michael Kay. *XSLT 2.0. Programmer's Reference*. Wiley Publishing, 2004.

[Kay08] Michael Kay. Ten Reasons Why Saxon XQuery is Fast. *IEEE Data Eng. Bull.*, 31(4):65–74, 2008.

[Kir10] Lukas Kircher. Extending a native XML database with XQuery Update. Bachelor's Thesis, University of Konstanz, Germany, October 2010.

[KKN03] Rajasekar Krishnamurthy, Raghav Kaushik, and Jeffrey F. Naughton. XML-SQL Query Translation Literature: The State of the Art and Open Problems. In *XSym*, volume 2824 of *Lecture Notes in Computer Science*, pages 1–18. Springer, 2003.

[KM00] Carl-Christian Kanne and Guido Moerkotte. Efficient Storage of XML Data. In *ICDE*, pages 198–218. IEEE Computer Society, 2000.

Bibliography

[Knu68] Donald E. Knuth. *The Art of Computer Programming, Volume I: Fundamental Algorithms*. Addison-Wesley, 1968.

[Knu73] Donald E. Knuth. *The Art of Computer Programming, Volume III: Sorting and Searching*. Addison-Wesley, 1973.

[Lev66] Vladimir I. Levenshtein. Binary codes capable of correcting deletions, insertions, and reversals. *Soviet Physics Doklady*, 10:707–710, 1966.

[Lew51] Kurt Lewin. *Field theory in social science: Selected theoretical papers*. Harper, 1951.

[LM01] Quanzhong Li and Bongki Moon. Indexing and Querying XML Data for Regular Path Expressions. In *VLDB*, pages 361–370. Morgan Kaufmann, 2001.

[LM03] Andreas Laux and Lars Martin. XUpdate – XML Update Language Working Draft. http://xmldb-org.sourceforge.net/xupdate/xupdate-wd.html, 2003.

[MAG+97] Jason McHugh, Serge Abiteboul, Roy Goldman, Dallan Quass, and Jennifer Widom. Lore: A Database Management System for Semistructured Data. *SIGMOD Record*, 26(3):54–66, 1997.

[MB04] David Megginson and David Brownell. SAX – Simple API for XML. http://www.saxproject.org, 2004.

[Mei02] Wolfgang Meier. eXist: An Open Source Native XML Database. In *Web, Web-Services, and Database Systems*, volume 2593 of *Lecture Notes in Computer Science*, pages 169–183. Springer, 2002.

[MMW07] Ashok Malhotra, Jim Melton, and Norman Walsh. XQuery 1.0 and XPath 2.0 Functions and Operators. http://www.w3.org/TR/xpath-functions, January 2007.

[Mor68] Donald R. Morrison. PATRICIA - Practical Algorithm To Retrieve Information Coded in Alphanumeric. *J. ACM*, 15(4):514–534, 1968.

[MW99] Jason McHugh and Jennifer Widom. Query Optimization for XML. In Atkinson et al. [AOV+99], pages 315–326.

[MWA+98] Jason McHugh, Jennifer Widom, Serge Abiteboul, Qingshan Luo, and Anand Rajaraman. Indexing semistructured data. Technical Report, Stanford University, Stanford, CA, 1998.

Bibliography

[OMFB02] Dan Olteanu, Holger Meuss, Tim Furche, and François Bry. XPath: Looking Forward. In *EDBT Workshops*, volume 2490 of *Lecture Notes in Computer Science*, pages 109–127. Springer, 2002.

[OOP+04] Patrick E. O'Neil, Elizabeth J. O'Neil, Shankar Pal, Istvan Cseri, Gideon Schaller, and Nigel Westbury. ORDPATHs: Insert-Friendly XML Node Labels. In Weikum et al. [WKD04], pages 903–908.

[PGMW95] Yannis Papakonstantinou, Hector Garcia-Molina, and Jennifer Widom. Object Exchange Across Heterogeneous Information Sources. In *ICDE*, pages 251–260. IEEE Computer Society, 1995.

[PMC02] Chang-Won Park, Jun-Ki Min, and Chin-Wan Chung. Structural Function Inlining Technique for Structurally Recursive XML Queries. In Bernstein et al. [BIRP02], pages 83–94.

[RLS98] Jonathan Robie, Joe Lapp, and David Schach. XML Query Language (XQL). In *QL*, 1998.

[RM01] Flavio Rizzolo and Alberto O. Mendelzon. Indexing XML Data with ToXin. In *WebDB*, pages 49–54, 2001.

[Rod03] Henning Rode. Methods and Cost Models for XPath Query Processing in Main Memory Databases. Master's thesis, University of Konstanz, Germany, October 2003.

[SCCS09] Haw Su-Cheng and Lee Chien-Sing. Node Labeling Schemes in XML Query Optimization: A Survey and Trends. *IETE Technical Review*, 26(2):88–100, 2009.

[SHS04] Gargi M. Sur, Joachim Hammer, and Jérôme Siméon. An XQuery-Based Language for Processing Updates in XML. In *PLAN-X*, number NS-03-4 in BRICS Notes Series, Venice, Italy, 2004.

[STZ+99] Jayavel Shanmugasundaram, Kristin Tufte, Chun Zhang, Gang He, David J. DeWitt, and Jeffrey F. Naughton. Relational Databases for Querying XML Documents: Limitations and Opportunities. In Atkinson et al. [AOV+99], pages 302–314.

[SWK+02] Albrecht Schmidt, Florian Waas, Martin L. Kersten, Michael J. Carey, Ioana Manolescu, and Ralph Busse. XMark: A Benchmark for XML Data Management. In Bernstein et al. [BIRP02], pages 974–985.

Bibliography

[TIHW01] Igor Tatarinov, Zachary G. Ives, Alon Y. Halevy, and Daniel S. Weld. Updating XML. In *SIGMOD Conference*, pages 413–424, 2001.

[TS04] Andrew Trotman and Börkur Sigurbjörnsson. Narrowed Extended XPath I (NEXI). In *INEX*, volume 3493 of *Lecture Notes in Computer Science*, pages 16–40. Springer, 2004.

[TVB+02] Igor Tatarinov, Stratis Viglas, Kevin S. Beyer, Jayavel Shanmugasundaram, Eugene J. Shekita, and Chun Zhang. Storing and Querying Ordered XML Using a Relational Database System. In Franklin et al. [FMA02], pages 204–215.

[TW02] Anja Theobald and Gerhard Weikum. The XXL search engine: Ranked Retrieval of XML data using Indexes and Ontologies. In Franklin et al. [FMA02], page 615.

[Ukk85] Esko Ukkonen. Algorithms for Approximate String Matching. *Information and Control*, 64(1-3):100–118, 1985.

[Vee09] Rolf Veen. OGDL – Ordered Graph Data Language. http://www.ogdl.org, 2009.

[vZAW99] Roelof van Zwol, Peter M. G. Apers, and Annita N. Wilschut. Modelling and Querying Semistructured Data with MOA. In *In proceedings of Workshop on Query Processing for Semistructured Data and Non-standard Data Formats*, 1999.

[Wei09] Rob Weir. OpenDocument Format: The Standard for Office Documents. *IEEE Internet Computing*, 13(2):83–87, 2009.

[Wei10] Andreas Weiler. Client-/Server-Architektur in XML Datenbanken. Master's thesis, University of Konstanz, Germany, September 2010.

[WG09] G. N. Wikramanayake and J. S. Goonetillake. Managing Very Large Databases and Data Warehousing. *Sri Lankan Journal on Librarianship and Information Management*, 2(1):22–29, 2009.

[Wir77] Niklaus Wirth. What Can We Do about the Unnecessary Diversity of Notation for Syntactic Definitions. *CACM*, 20(11):822–823, 1977.

Bibliography

[WK06] Utz Westermann and Wolfgang Klas. PTDOM: a Schema-Aware XML Database System for MPEG-7 Media Descriptions. *Softw., Pract. Exper.*, 36(8):785–834, 2006.

[WKD04] Gerhard Weikum, Arnd Christian König, and Stefan Deßloch, editors. *Proceedings of the ACM SIGMOD International Conference on Management of Data, Paris, France, June 13-18, 2004*. ACM, 2004.

[WMB99] Ian H. Witten, Alistair Moffat, and Timothy C. Bell. *Managing Gigabytes: Compressing and Indexing Documents and Images, Second Edition*. Morgan Kaufmann, 1999.

List of Figures

2.1 Preorder, postorder, and inorder traversal 8
2.2 XML document, tree with $pre/post$ values, $pre/post$ plane 9
2.3 Bitwise distribution of node properties in BASEX 6.0. Note: the ns bit is located to the right of the uri property 22
2.4 Directory of logical pages: a) initial state for a page size of 4096 bytes, b) deletion of 100 nodes, and c) insertion of 100 nodes 24
2.5 Main structure of a database instance 25
2.6 Class diagram for building a database with a SAX parser 26
2.7 Class diagram: extended architecture for database construction 30
2.8 XML document, tree representation, path summary incl. cardinalities . . . 34
2.9 Trie representation of the XML sample document 41

3.1 Class diagram with expression types 52
3.2 Query with a function declaration, variables, arithmetic expressions, and a conditional branch 58
3.3 Type hierarchy of the XML Data Model [FMM+07] 59
3.4 XML document, tree representation, summary, and path expressions 60
3.5 FLWOR expression: original and optimized query 64
3.6 $pre/post$ planes; *descendant* step for the three A elements: a) conventional, b) with Pruning, c) with Partitioning, d) with Skipping 84
3.7 Class diagram: location path expressions 86
3.8 Query 1 & 2: Path expressions with equality comparison 100
3.9 Query 3: FLWOR expression with equality comparison 101
3.10 XMark Query 1: Original and optimized query plan 102
3.11 XMark Query 7: Original query plan 103
3.12 XMark Query 9: Optimized/original query plan (top/bottom) 104
3.13 (Inofficial) XMark Query 21: Optimized/original query plan 105

List of Figures

4.1 Database creation of XMark instances with BASEX. Left: single times for database and index creation, right: total time on different architectures . . 108
4.2 Database creation of various smaller XML instances (Sources: Table 4.5) . 109
4.3 XMark documents: build times and database sizes 109
4.4 Bulk vs. incremental database creation (NEWYORKTIMES documents) . . . 111
4.5 Basic XQuery expressions: comparison of different processors. DNF: did not finish within 5 min. 113
4.6 Advanced XQuery expressions: comparison of different processors. ERR: could not be evaluated, DNF: did not finish within 5 min. 115
4.7 Opening a 111MB XMark document in main memory 117
4.8 Processing four queries on an 11MB XMark instance. DNF: did not finish within 5 min. 117
4.9 Processing all XMark queries on a 111MB XMark instance. DNF: did not finish within 5 min. 118
4.10 XMark Queries: Scalability of BASEX. DNF: did not finish within 60 min. . 120
4.11 XMark Queries: Version history of BASEX. DNF: did not finish within 5 min. 121
4.12 XMark Queries: Comparing BASEX 6.3 with results in [GHK+06]. DNF: did not finish within 5 min. 122
4.13 English Wikipedia: Processing times and result sizes of seven full-text queries and six search terms 127
4.14 English Wikipedia: Processing times and result sizes of seven advanced full-text queries 128

List of Tables

2.1	Summary of node properties (✓: fixed size, +: variable size)	13
2.2	Summary of normalized node properties. +/−: large/small address space, c: constant value	17
2.3	Value ranges for XML documents and collections. See Table 4.5 for a complete survey	18
2.4	Bits needed to allocate value ranges	20
2.5	Concrete bit ranges for all node kinds	21
2.6	Compression of numeric values. b represents a bit, B represents a byte	36
2.7	Fuzzy Index instance, sorted by token length and lexicographical order	39
2.8	Trie Index instance, tabular representation	40
3.1	Comparison between SQL and XQL (taken from [RLS98])	44
4.1	Hardware architectures used for testing	107
4.2	Compared XQuery processors (standalone, client-/server architecture)	111
4.3	Usual runtimes for evaluating an empty sequence (15 runs)	112
4.4	Wikipedia: Ranking results of Query $Q6$, compared with a Google query	129
4.5	Statistics on selected XML documents and collections	131
4.6	References to document sources (last accessed: 1 Oct 2010)	132

I want morebooks!

Buy your books fast and straightforward online - at one of world's fastest growing online book stores! Environmentally sound due to Print-on-Demand technologies.

Buy your books online at
www.morebooks.shop

Kaufen Sie Ihre Bücher schnell und unkompliziert online – auf einer der am schnellsten wachsenden Buchhandelsplattformen weltweit! Dank Print-On-Demand umwelt- und ressourcenschonend produziert.

Bücher schneller online kaufen
www.morebooks.shop

KS OmniScriptum Publishing
Brivibas gatve 197
LV-1039 Riga, Latvia
Telefax: +371 686 204 55

info@omniscriptum.com
www.omniscriptum.com

Printed by Books on Demand GmbH, Norderstedt / Germany